Dedicated to the revealing of God's glory
through Jesus Christ
and
to Barbara,
who has loved and
believed in me.

FOREWORD BY JAY KESLER

FINDING YOUR WAY HOME

FREEING THE CHILD WITHIN YOU AND DISCOVERING WHOLENESS IN THE FUNCTIONAL FAMILY OF GOD

KENNETH A. SCHMIDT

Regal Books
A Division of Gospel Light
Ventura, California, U.S.A.

Published by Regal Books
A Division of Gospel Light
Ventura, California 93006
Printed in U.S.A.

Library of Congress Cataloging-in-Publication Data
Schmidt, Kenneth A.
>Finding your way home: freeing the child within you and discovering wholeness in the functional family of God / Kenneth A. Schmidt.
>p. cm.
>ISBN 0-8307-1394-8
>1. Freedom (Theology)   2. Sin.   3. Salvation.   4. Mental health—Religious aspects—Christianity.   5. Christian life—1960-
>I. Title.
>BT810.2.S26 1990
>234—dc20
>   90-26496
>   CIP

2 3 4 5 6 7 8 9 10 / KP / X3.0 / 95 94 93 92 91

Rights for publishing this book in other languages are contracted by Gospel Literature International (GLINT). GLINT also provides technical help for the adaptation, translation, and publishing of Bible study resources and books in scores of languages worldwide. For further information, contact GLINT, Post Office Box 488, Rosemead, California, 91770, U.S.A., or the publisher.

FINDING YOUR WAY HOME

A MUCH-NEEDED BLENDING OF THEOLOGY WITH PSYCHOLOGY
AND SPIRITUALITY WITH THERAPY. IF WE HAD MORE
COUNSELORS LIKE KEN SCHMIDT WE'D HAVE A LOT MORE
PEOPLE BEING HEALED.

ROBERT HUDNUT
SENIOR PASTOR, WINNETKA PRESBYTERIAN CHURCH
AUTHOR OF *MEETING GOD IN THE DARKNESS*

FINDING YOUR WAY HOME IS AN EXCELLENT RESOURCE FOR
ASSISTING INDIVIDUALS TO COME TO GRIPS WITH DIFFICULT
ISSUES IN THEIR LIVES. THOSE INTERESTED IN RESOLVING
PERSONAL AND FAMILY CONFLICTS WILL ENJOY THIS
EXCELLENT RESOURCE.

BOB PHILLIPS, PH.D.
DIRECTOR, HUME LAKE CHRISTIAN CAMPS

CONTENTS

FOREWORD

ONE can scarcely pick up a newspaper or magazine these days without being reminded of the tragic condition of the family in the modern world. Much advice is available from both a secular and Christian perspective and, in given situations, most of it is good and will help. Still, the problem of family turmoil doesn't seem to decrease.

With *Finding Your Way Home*, however, I believe Ken Schmidt has made an important contribution. He asks us to compare our family patterns and presuppositions on which we base our conduct, not on one another, with television models, or alternate approaches, but with the Bible and the principles of the Christian faith.

This process of self-examination often involves a complete rebuilding of fondly held biases and a willingness to come to God in humility to allow a complete transformation of all that we are and even the pathways that have led us to our present state. The process often sounds radical and the ideal seems unattainable, yet without a careful analysis of God's master plan, it is unlikely that we will put our lives together successfully from a basket of borrowed secular spare parts.

In *Finding Your Way Home* there are some challenging ideas to confront and many practical suggestions for bringing about solutions. We welcome this new book to the arsenal of God in the spiritual warfare for the family.

—Dr. Jay Kesler, President
Taylor University
Upland, Indiana

ACKNOWLEDGMENTS

THIS book would not have been written without the support, encouragement and deep involvement of my wife, Barbara. She has not only supported me, but also handled the more difficult task of disagreeing with me when I needed her perspective. Her walk with Christ has often opened my eyes and revealed Him in new ways.

I'm grateful to Bill Greig, Jr. and Billie Baptiste of Gospel Light for opening the door for the writing of this book. They helped make a dream come true.

My editors, Dr. Ron Durham and Kyle Duncan, have guided the efforts of a first-time author with a caring hand. I appreciate the kinship we've discovered and the friendships we've begun.

A number of people have helped by reviewing the book during its development. My wife, Barbara, and my daughter, Diane, have read every chapter and struggled to help me find words when they were elusive. Their questions, disagreements, suggestions and encouragement have been invaluable.

A special thanks to Lynne Farrow, Dave and Mary Ann Rohrer, Kit and Kris Donna Mack, Don Goehner, Nancy Kern, Audrey Black and Brent Ashby for reviewing portions of the book and giving me honest feedback. Their efforts meant a lot to me when I was still finding my way.

Thanks also to my son, Mark, and my daughter, Karen, for their encouragement through times when they must have wearied of "the book" and our conversations about it.

Many of the ideas and perspectives for this book were developed while I was teaching the Clippers Adult Sunday School class at Community Presbyterian Church in Ventura. I'm grateful to the members of that class for their participation, their ideas and their feedback during our months together.

Finally, I thank those who have shared their lives and their pain with me as their therapist. These are the people who have contributed the most. I'm grateful that their courage and honesty have led to an understanding of Christ that would not have been possible without them.

—Ken Schmidt

INTRODUCTION:
BREAKING FREE

If you hold to my teaching, you are really my disciples. Then you will know the truth, and the truth will set you free.
—John 8:31,32

JESUS said, "The truth will set you free." Yet few of us experience the freedom He promises. When I became a therapist twelve years ago, I discovered that many Christians are living in misery rather than freedom and joy. They feel depressed and trapped in lives with little hope. Though they take their faith seriously and try to obey Christ, they're not really alive.

My life was like this for years. Christ's promises of life, joy and peace often seemed empty. Christian speakers said I shouldn't trust my emotions but should have faith in the facts and then the feelings would follow. That didn't work. My emotions were telling me something was missing. It was important to pay attention.

The turning point came as I began to understand relationships. Breaking free from damaging patterns of relating helped me relate to God. Realizing my freedom in Christ allowed me to become more honest and open so that I began to experience God more genuinely and intimately. As I trusted the person of Christ rather than the facts about Him, life blossomed.

I had tried to love God and feel loved by Him for years. When I honestly opened my heart instead, I received the warm love of Christ in addition to the cold facts of theology. When I revealed my emotions and trusted Him with who I am, He proved trustworthy. Christ has set me free, and He can do the same for you.

RECOGNIZING OUR SLAVERY

To be interested in breaking free, we must first recognize that slavery is at the root of the perpetual pain in our lives. We will see no use for the remedy if we don't first acknowledge the pain. The bad news must precede the good. When Jesus said, "You will know the truth, and the truth will set you free," His listeners replied, "We...have never been slaves of anyone" (John 8:33). By denying their slavery, they refused their freedom.

As a therapist, I work with people who have had their eyes opened to their slavery. They have recognized their pain and had the courage to face it. In beginning recovery, they realized their need of God's grace. Those of us

> *To be interested in breaking free, we must first recognize that slavery is at the root of the perpetual pain in our lives.*

who have not identified our pain need His grace in the same measure. We, too, must be set free from a slavery initiated before we were born and passed on to us as children.

If you have identified a need for recovery from childhood pain or abuse, or from problems of addiction, this book is intended to help you recover as part of your Christian faith. Many people develop doubts about their faith when they begin recovery in a non-Christian setting. Some decide to stop attending church and become confused about what it means to be a Christian. This is tragic, for our recovery is rooted in Jesus Christ. When we recognize how God's love through Christ can set us free, our faith becomes more alive and dynamic than it has ever been.

But maybe you're functioning well according to the standards of "normal" behavior and haven't recognized childhood pain or any need for recovery. You may have only wondered, *Is this all there is?* about your Christian experience. This is how I felt before I realized I was trying to relate to God in ways that didn't work. Living as a Christian requires learning new, loving ways to relate to God and each other. If you're looking for a deeper, more real experience of Christ, the perspective I offer will make a difference.

The healing work of Jesus Christ is psychologically sound. Psychology and theology will be interwoven throughout this book, because the process of recovery has to do with people (psychology) and with God (theology), not with one isolated from the other. Our use of the Bible has too often been separated from the reality of people's experience. When we understand people, we will more clearly understand the Bible and the One to whom it points.

WE ALL NEED RECOVERY

All of humanity is in need of recovery from sin. Today, we have the opportunity to understand this in a new way. Millions are experiencing recovery from addiction and painful childhoods through groups such as Alcoholics Anonymous (AA) and Adult Children of Alcoholics (ACA). Alcoholics Anonymous was begun in 1935 by two Christians who based their work on the Bible and their faith experience. These spiritually based groups are spreading rapidly throughout the world while the influence of the organized church has been declining.

I believe the Holy Spirit is communicating through the ministry of these groups. Their emphasis on vulnerability, honesty and openness is deeply needed for the recovery of vitality in the church. I've heard more than one person say, "AA has been to me what the church should have been." These are not statements of anger but of reality. The healing of these groups can help us refocus the life of the church. By learning from their ministries, we can cooperate with the work the Holy Spirit has already begun.

The ACA movement was started by people raised in homes where at least one parent was alcoholic. They discovered the alcoholic family's patterns of relating had caused similar problems in their adult relationships and attempts to cope with adult life. In order to benefit from one another's experience and support, they formed self-help groups following the AA format.

The people of ACA soon realized, however, that their problems were not unique to alcoholic families. Rather, they are common to everyone raised in a damaging family environment. This included adults who had experienced physical, sexual or emotional abuse as children. Thus, the organization eventually opened its doors to anyone identifying a need for recovery from childhood in a dysfunctional family.

> *When we become desperate enough to face the reality of our emotions, our relationships and our world, and entrust them to God, He breaks us free.*

A "dysfunctional family" may be defined as one that did not adequately prepare its children to function as adults, particularly in their relationships. By this definition, most families are dysfunctional to one extent or another, but dysfunction is easier to see when it occurs in the extreme. Those of us who cannot identify with being raised by an alcoholic mother or being beaten by an enraged father can believe, "I'm not like them; I had a good family." Nonetheless, though our experience may be less extreme, our need is no less real.

For this reason, I prefer my own definition: "A dysfunctional family is one that has hindered us from being who God created us to be." By this definition, all families are indeed dysfunctional. We're all recovering from painful experiences of growing up, because they're common to mankind. We are all in need of recovery.

But we need more than recovery. Jesus Christ came to confront us with the reality of our alienation from God the Father. That loss of relationship has led to our addiction and dysfunction. Christ came to redeem and restore us to relationships with God and each other.

Immediately after Jesus proclaimed, "You will know the truth, and the truth will set you free," His listeners not only claimed they weren't slaves, but also based their claim to freedom on their family. They said that because they were Abraham's children, they didn't need to be set free. Jesus pointed out that Abraham would not have rejected the truth as they were doing and that their true father was the devil. He emphasized that only those who belong to God the Father are free.

> I tell you the truth, everyone who sins is a slave to sin. Now a slave has no permanent place in the family, but a son belongs to it forever. So if the Son sets you free, you will be free indeed....If God were your Father, you would love me, for I came from God and now am here. I have not come on my own; but he sent me....If I am telling the truth, why don't you believe me? He who belongs to God hears what God says. The reason you do not hear is that you do not belong to God (John 8:34-36,42,46,47).

Jesus Christ came to bring us into the family of God. If we cling to the dysfunctional patterns of our human families, however, we remain slaves. To be free, we must shift our loyalty from our dysfunctional families to God. As His children, we have a permanent place in His family, and that security gives us the freedom to live.

Jesus not only said the truth would set us free, but He then proceeded to speak, live and be the truth we need for freedom. We rejoice at Jesus' words. We want the freedom. Do we want the truth? The truth brings pain before it brings freedom, the pain of carrying our cross and following Jesus, trusting the promise of the Resurrection.

Miraculously, resurrection does occur. When we become

desperate enough to face the reality of our emotions, our relationships and our world and entrust them to God, He breaks us free. We then begin to experience the joy and the peace Christ promised even in the midst of pain and suffering. Life becomes an adventure to experience rather than a frustration to be endured. We discover ourselves becoming whole and experiencing life more fully. We haven't yet arrived, but we've come to trust the One we're following. The goal of this book is to suggest ways in which you can make such discoveries yourself.

USING THE PERSONAL REFLECTION SECTIONS

At the end of each chapter, you'll find a section entitled "For Personal Reflection." These sections suggest activities or study you may pursue to learn more about the topic(s) of that chapter. At the back of the book, in a special section, I recommend books for further reading.

If you have begun recovery from childhood pain, I strongly encourage you to read some of the excellent books on dysfunctional families, codependency and recovery. My goal in this book is not to explain those issues in detail, but to provide a Christian perspective on them. Additional reading will add much depth to your understanding and further your growth. You will learn that our faith in Christ is consistent with the recovery process described in most of those books.

If you have already done much reading and recovery work and my Christian viewpoint on it is new to you, I encourage you to read the books I recommend on the Christian faith, especially those by C. S. Lewis. As a devotional guide consistent with the perspective I'm sharing, I strongly recommend *My Utmost for His Highest,* by Oswald Chambers.

PART ONE

THE DYSFUNCTIONAL HUMAN FAMILY: OUR SLAVERY TO SIN

TO BECOME LIKE A CHILD

THE BEGINNINGS OF OUR PERSONAL SLAVERY TO SIN

Anyone who loves his father or mother more than me is not worthy of me; anyone who loves his son or daughter more than me is not worthy of me.
—Matthew 10:37

CHRIST UNITED METHODIST CHURCH
4488 POPLAR AVENUE
MEMPHIS, TENNESSEE 38117

Mary was an attractive young woman who had recently graduated from college. She had done well in her studies, been offered an excellent job, and was clearly capable. Though she seemed to have everything going for her, she'd been living in pain and confusion for years without telling anyone. Why had she remained silent?

Mary was frightened as she told her story. "I shouldn't feel so miserable. My parents were good to me. They've never beaten or abused me. We always had food on the table. There must be something wrong with me." Mary saw her parents as good and had always worked to be obedient. Her parents were proud of her goodness.

As we talked, I asked her if she felt depressed. When I described depression, she said, "I can't feel that way. I'm a Christian." When I said Christians get depressed, too, she began to cry.

Mary's mother had been domineering. Because theirs was a Christian family and prominent in the church, everybody was to be loving and happy. If the children were ever angry or unloving, they would be scolded and told to change. They were taught that God loved them, so they should never feel unhappy, afraid, unloved or angry. It was in fact sinful to feel sad or depressed, for the Bible says Christians are to be joyful.

In response, Mary worked to be a happy, friendly child, always smiling and apparently enjoying life. When she felt anger or hurt, she concluded something was wrong with her and pushed the feelings away. Literally hundreds of times she had heard her mother say, when she looked less than cheerful, "Is that the face a Christian wears?" She became ashamed of her true feelings and had spent a lifetime with them trapped inside her in the name of Jesus Christ.

Under pressure to be joyful, victorious and unafraid, Mary was none of those things. God had created her to feel her own feelings, think her own thoughts, speak her own words, and create her own creations. She was meant to become a unique human being. But Mary's Christian family was dysfunctional because it had prevented that.

We are to love Jesus Christ more than we love our families. These are hard words. Our parents are all we have when we're born, and we've depended on them to protect, feed and teach us. Most of our parents tried hard to do what they believed was best. We learned what love means and how to live our lives from them. They've also taught us who we are and who God is. During our earliest years they were our gods, for we couldn't live without them. *Our families are the most powerful tools the world has used to shape us.*

But human beings are not good gods. Even in the best of families, we've learned much that is not true. Our parents usually didn't intend to hurt us, but, in spite of their good intentions, they did. And now, because our parents were gods to us, we must shift our ultimate loyalty away from them.

We are to love Jesus more than our families because that's the only way to be free. When Scripture tells us to "not conform any longer to the pattern of this world" (Rom. 12:2), that includes refusing to remain in the worldly patterns impressed on us by our families.

We must "leave" our families emotionally and spiritually and start life over again.

> I tell you the truth, unless a man is born again, he cannot see the kingdom of God (John 3:3).
> I tell you the truth, unless you change and become like

little children, you will never enter the kingdom of heaven (Matthew 18:3).

Christians shouldn't be surprised that families are dysfunctional. It's basic to our theology that human beings don't function as God intends. So to say that our families often don't function in healthy ways should not be news.

Yet many, like Mary, refuse to admit they've been harmed by their families. In some Christian circles, the family is even considered sacred and not to be criticized for any reason. Others fear that speaking honestly about family problems is dishonoring to their parents. They don't want to appear ungrateful, so they deny their pain. They believe, without realizing it, that dishonestly protecting parents is more honoring than speaking the truth in love. These very beliefs are part of their family dysfunction.

To speak honestly about the failings of families may seem negative and damaging. It is not. Confessing their dysfunction does not rob them of significance or honor but opens them to recovery. Healthy individuals confess and responsibly face problems. Healthy families do, too.

We were created to be God's children. Because Adam and Eve broke the relationship with Him millennia ago, we became incapable of loving children as they need to be loved. No matter how loving parents are, they simply can't love the way God intends. As a result we don't receive the love we were created for, and we can't become all that God created us to be. Consequently, as we interact with the world as children, we lose our souls, our true selves. The idea that human beings possess a "true self" that is somehow hidden and yet very real is consistent with New Testament teaching. The words most frequently used to denote what I'm calling the "true self" are *psyche* or "soul," and *kardia*, or "heart." "Psyche" is the root of the word "psychology." The soul is the "inward man," distinguishing us as unique persons. It is the result of God's creation of us as individuals.[1] The *kardia* is used for the "hidden man" or "real man."[2]

Thus our need for a new family. In addition to loving us in ways our human families did not, it must deal with the damage done in our childhood. We must shift our primary loyalty from our human families to this new family, the family of God.

> Then Jesus entered a house, and again a crowd gathered, so that he and his disciples were not even able to eat. When his family heard about this, they went to take charge of him, for they said, "He is out of his mind."...
>
> Standing outside, they sent someone in to call him. A crowd was sitting around him, and they told him, "Your mother and brothers are outside looking for you."
>
> "Who are my mother and my brothers?" he asked.
>
> Then he looked at those seated in a circle around him and said, "Here are my mother and my brothers! Whoever does God's will is my brother and sister and mother" (Mark 3:20-21,31-35).

When I first read this, I thought Jesus was being cruel. Now I realize He's right. We can't enter into and enjoy our relationship with our heavenly Father without spiritually changing families. We are now brothers and sisters with all who follow Jesus.

Jesus Christ experienced the cross so you and I could become whole, recover our true selves, and experience the joy of life. Through Jesus, God relates to us very differently from the way our parents did. As we break free from the dysfunctional relationship patterns of our families and discover a true relationship with God, we recover our lost souls. The beginning point is to understand how we lose them in the first place.

SHAME BEGINS OUR SLAVERY TO SIN

Children are born without shame. They cry when they feel like crying, scream when they're angry, and laugh when they want to laugh. They have no sense that it's wrong for them to feel what they feel and express it. They're dependent; they're vulnerable; they're powerless, they're in complete poverty. They have nothing unless it's given to them, and they feel no shame about their need. They simply are who they are.

This doesn't last long, however. Soon human expectations and judgment accomplish something God never intended. They become ashamed of who they are. And our experience of slavery to sin begins with the development of shame about ourselves. But shame is so much a part of what it is to be human that we're as unaware of it as we are of breathing. We Christians would like to believe this isn't true of Christian families, but it often is. Mary's family is a prime example.

Jesus was inviting hurting girls like Mary when He said, "Let the little children come to me, and do not hinder them" (Luke 18:16). Her family had taught her that feelings should not be revealed. They had hindered her from bringing those feelings to Jesus, for she was ashamed of them.

Mary's shame may be difficult to understand, since we don't use the word "shame" often in everyday conversation and can confuse it with guilt. But here's the difference: I feel guilty when I've *done* something I believe I shouldn't. I feel shame when I believe I *am* someone I shouldn't *be*. Guilt is about what I do, while shame is about who I am.

We feel ashamed of revealing the parts of us we believe should not exist. We don't want them exposed. Mary was ashamed of her feelings because she had been taught they were "bad." The child within her had received the same answer Charlie Brown receives from Lucy in figure 1.

We all want what Charlie Brown desires. We could say with Lucy, "Sure, I understand perfectly." We want to know we're special, that people like us and enjoy being with us. We want to know that it isn't only all right to be ourselves but that people will *rejoice* in who we are. We want others to be joyful with

Figure 1

us when we're joyful and to mourn with us when we're mournful (see Rom. 12:15). We want to be valued.

Yet Lucy's response is what we all experience to some degree. We're taught to forget it, to give up our hope of being loved as we are and to set aside our pain to survive. We conclude we're worthless and begin to feel ashamed. Rather than rejoicing in who we are, we have to hide, for we don't fit the expectations of the adult world.

This kind of shame is a fundamental characteristic of a dysfunctional family. The interactions that occur between individuals rest on the underlying conviction that we can't reveal how we really think or feel, for it's bad. The shame prevents honest interaction and people learn to live according to rules and to play roles, rather than being free to be themselves.

How Shame Develops

Thousands of events in childhood combine to convince us there is something wrong with our feelings and desires. Most of these events don't seem traumatic to adults, yet they affect us as children in subtle yet powerful ways.

Consider four-year-old Johnny. He wants pancakes for breakfast. He bounds out of bed in the morning and into the kitchen, where his mother is drinking coffee and trying to wake herself up. Johnny is pure energy, as alive as he can be, looking forward to being with his mother and having the pancakes he loves. He is all child.

Mom hears Johnny calling out for pancakes and inwardly groans. The last thing she wants to do is prepare pancakes. If she weren't burdened by shame herself, she might simply say, "No, I don't want to cook pancakes today. Have some cereal instead." Johnny would feel disappointed and maybe angry. But after eating his cereal, the event would be forgotten, and both Mom and Johnny could go on without carrying shame.

Yet shame is such a pervasive part of a dysfunctional family that a simple experience like Johnny's wanting pancakes can turn into an emotional disaster. If Mom is dominated by feelings of shame, she will tell herself within. "You're a bad mother. You should want to fix pancakes for your son." But she'll hide the shame from Johnny and herself. Instead of admitting she doesn't want to cook pancakes, she may say, "All you ever think about is yourself! You think I should give you pancakes whenever you want them!" She shifts the blame to Johnny, implying that Johnny should not want what he wants.

Johnny has not *done* anything wrong, but Mother is saying something *arising from inside him is wrong:* his desires. If Johnny is a healthy little boy, he will be confused by her response. He was hoping for a time with Mom and some pancakes, and now he's being accused of being selfish. *He will believe this message.* Mom is a god to him, and he has no alternative but to believe her. As the accusation sinks in, he may begin to cry—not because he's not getting pancakes but because he feels so bad about himself. If Mom now feels guilty, she may proceed with the clincher: "You think you have something to cry about? I'll give you something to cry about!" And then she spanks him.

What has Johnny learned? That he has desires he shouldn't have. He feels ashamed that he wanted pancakes and time with his mom. He has also learned that he has bad feelings. He was spanked for crying. He feels ashamed that he felt ashamed and hurt.

Johnny has learned not to trust his wants or his feelings. Now he must learn to evaluate which things he should want or not want and which feelings he should feel or not feel *according to someone else's rules.* He must judge whether what he wants or feels is good or bad so as to stay safe from criticism. Eventually these rules will be internalized, and then he won't need Mother to judge him but will do it himself.

A simple situation where a child wants pancakes and Mom

doesn't want to provide them thus moves from being a short-lived disappointment to a lifetime question of personal value. Instead of "I don't get pancakes today," it becomes "I had better be careful, because there are desires and feelings inside me that are evil. I can't trust what I think or feel." The real child is being hidden away.

All of us parents can recognize this mother's reaction in ourselves. As I was writing this, my daughter asked for help with homework. I responded in irritation with, "You should do it yourself," and walked away. I later realized her request was reasonable but I didn't want to help her. I had blamed her for wanting rather than honestly saying, "No I don't want to help you now." I was ashamed to be honest because I believed a good father should always help his child with homework. My response could lead her to feel ashamed of wanting or needing help.

Physical and emotional abuse of children follows this same pattern. Something a child says or does leads a parent to feel upset. The parent responds by punishing the child for creating the feeling. The child who is being abused is forcefully being told, "You are of no value" and "You should not be who you are." The part of the child that angered the parent is now experienced as worthless and hidden. If the child cried and the parent reacted abusively to the crying, the child further learns to feel ashamed of the hurt and tears. If the child expressed anger and the parent's response was abuse, the child also hides the anger within.

The most destructive shame develops when parents act out deeply hostile feelings on their children. This intensely painful rejection and abuse forces kids to conclude they are deeply flawed. At a young age, they can't consider the possibility that their parents are responsible for their pain. The pain can only be explained as due to some horrible lack in themselves.

SHAME CAUSED BY JUDGMENT

Judgment is what leads to shame. Johnny's desire for pancakes was judged as bad because his mother didn't want to prepare them. His tears were judged as bad because his mother felt guilty when she saw them.

I'm using the words "judge" and "judgment" throughout this book to refer to judgments made on people's value, or "goodness." I'm not referring to our ability to make a decision or choose a course of action, because making a decision doesn't necessarily include determining the value of a person or thing. I would rather be a therapist than an attorney. This is a decision I made in determining my life's direction. That's different from saying therapists are *better* than attorneys. One kind of judgment is simply a statement of preference. The other is a determination of worth. The kind of judgment leading to shame is that which states we are of less worth than another or are "bad."

I have strong feelings about judgment. After twelve years as a therapist, I see it as a consistent theme running through the problems of humanity. This is not God's judgment of human beings but the judgment of human beings upon each other and themselves. As a beginning therapist, there were days when I felt overwhelmed by the damage I saw in people's lives and relationships because of judgment.

I have seen individuals reveal judgments of their marriage partners as wrong, unloving or inadequate. I have seen their partners react to these judgments by judging them in return. These judgments are often subtle and cloaked with the best of intentions, yet from outside the marriage they're clear. I have also begun to realize my own patterns of judging my wife and working to "straighten her out." My attitude too often implies, "You're good when you do what I want." I would never verbalize it that boldly, but I send that message much of the time.

In individual therapy, I've seen the judgments of parents on their children in the pain of my clients' childhoods. Their parents judged them as inadequate in appearance, intelligence or behavior, and those "loving" attempts to change them into more valuable people (for them) have crippled them. They now continue to judge themselves as their parents judged them.

> *All judgment hurts, but the most powerful judgments about our value are those we receive when we're most vulnerable—during our earliest childhood.*

In contrast, we may have been judged as desirable or good. We may have been praised for our appearance or our abilities so that our parents would feel good about themselves. Their decision to judge us positively and to use us unconsciously for their gain may seem like a gift, but it is a curse that can haunt us for life. It sends the message that our value is based on the characteristic they desired for themselves.

The young girl whose attractiveness is focused on may spend her life working at being attractive and fearing that if she isn't, she will no longer be loved. She wasn't valued as a whole human being but specifically for her beauty. When it fades due to age or injury, she may have great difficulty expressing and enjoying the rest of her humanity.

The young child who is judged as valuable because of his competence may seem to be receiving a gift. Yet he may become an adult workaholic without realizing he's doing it to maintain his sense of worth. And his enjoyment of life will fade into depression when those skills deteriorate.

Self-esteem based on our performance, appearance or any other human characteristic can actually rob us of the opportunity to simply enjoy being alive. In their proper perspective, these characteristics can bring great joy, but if we're treated as though they *create* our worth, we have been damaged by human judgment.

From the moment of birth, our worth as human beings is constantly evaluated according to our skin color, our sex, our abilities, our social standing, our nationality, and on and on and on. All judgment hurts, but the most powerful judgments about our value are those we receive when we're most vulnerable—during our earliest childhood. These judgments leave the greatest sense of shame and result in the greatest loss of self.

SHAME AND DEVELOPMENT

Judgment and shame are incredibly powerful when we're very young because we're still being created at that time. An infant is not yet aware of being a self. You may have seen the miracle of the baby "discovering" her hands. She looks at them, touches them, and is fascinated by the realization that she has some control over what they do. We also must discover our selves and the fact that there are other selves as well. The two-year-old who says no is discovering he has a will separate from that of his parents. He doesn't know this when he's born. We are still "in process" throughout childhood, still "being created." Unfortunately, grown-ups seldom realize this and treat children as little adults.

My unthinking treatment of children as adults was demonstrated when I was playing catch with my three-year-old daughter. She was having trouble catching the ball, so I, the coach, told her, "Keep your eye on the ball!" She proceeded to toddle over to the ball, pick it up, and hold it squarely against her eyeball!

Unfortunately, the results aren't always humorous. I also believed my daughter should share her toys when she was two, because that was the "good" thing to do. I wanted her to be a good child so everyone would know what a good parent I was. I didn't know she was still learning she was a person.

She was just realizing it was possible to say, "Mine!" when I was forcing her to share. Children can't learn to share until they know they are capable of possessing. My lack of respect for her developing self could cause her to feel ashamed of her desires.

Much of this continuing creation during childhood has been studied and can be predicted fairly accurately. My wife is a reading specialist. It's important for her to determine a child's stage of development because it affects his ability to learn to read. If he hasn't reached the appropriate developmental level, all the help in the world won't enable him to read.

If people judge kids as poor readers because they can't read after the first grade, they may be ignoring the fact that they haven't yet become who they will be. The judgment may create a lasting shame about their intelligence, though they may be capable of reading given additional time.

The tragedy for the most severely abused or neglected children is that they don't develop a sense of self. The tragedy for us all is that we lose parts of ourselves—physical, spiritual and emotional—because we're convinced these parts are worthless. For instance, the child who is judged as evil because she touches her genitals is often just discovering they are there! Many women have never looked at their genitals because of this lifelong shame. We must learn to respect the fact that God is creating each of us from within even after we're born.

How Are We Judged?

Our worth is evaluated by others according to *their needs*. Those parts they don't need and so reject are the parts we hide in shame. Dr. Alice Miller's pioneering study of child abuse and neglect can help us understand the tragic impact of life in a sin-damaged world. She wrote, "Sometimes I ask myself whether it will ever be possible for us to grasp the extent of the loneliness and desertion to which we were exposed as children and hence (within ourselves) are exposed to as adults."[3]

Dr. Miller concludes that we're damaged as children when we're born into a world of damaged adults. These adults have deep, unrecognized needs that they try to fill through their relationships with their children.

> Parents who did not experience [the love they needed] as children are themselves deprived; throughout their lives they are looking for what their parents could not give them at the correct time—the presence of a person who is completely aware of them and takes them seriously....
>
> A person with this unsatisfied and unconscious need is compelled to attempt its gratification through substitute means. The most [available] objects for gratification are a parents' own children.[4]

You may object to this by saying, "I don't expect my child to meet my needs." Keep in mind, however, that the needs I'm describing are *disowned* needs. Parents aren't consciously aware of their needs nor are they aware of the messages they send. The Little League father doesn't realize he's trying to live his life through his son, though it may be painfully apparent to others. The mother slapping her boy for being noisy in the grocery store doesn't know she's punishing him for not maintaining her positive image. The dad who is disappointed when his daughter doesn't play the violin seldom understands his own desire for recognition.

I'm not saying all interactions between parents and children occur only for the good of the parents. To the extent parents had their needs met in childhood, they are able to give to their own children. We look to our children to try to fill the "holes" in our own being; to heal the hurts or fill the emptiness remaining from our early years. The greater our need, the more likely we are to turn to our children to fill it.

We don't look only to our children to meet our needs. We also put these expectations on our other relationships, especially our spouses. Recognizing the unmet emotional needs we expect others to fill requires much personal growth and painful honesty on our part. In therapy, people often realize for the first time the role they have given their children when they face their own early pain and need. Once a loss is faced and mourned, we will no longer look to our children to fill it.

> *Fault and blame are so much a part of our lives that it's difficult to deal with childhood pain without blaming our parents. It's also true that many people do not get beyond this point in their growth.*

Another likely objection at this point could be, "But children don't meet their parents' needs. In fact, many of them seem to do the exact opposite." There are at least three reasons for this.

First, some children meet their parents' needs by being "bad." An example is the mother who was severely criticized for failing to meet her parents' need for order. She will hate the "messy" child within her. To handle her self-loathing, she needs someone outside her to whom to transfer the blame. Her own daughter can unconsciously serve this purpose. Mother sends two messages to accomplish this: (1) you must be neat and orderly, (2) you are sloppy and are therefore failing me.

The daughter will believe these messages and fail in her attempts to be neat. And Mother, rather than experiencing the feelings of the vulnerable, hurting child within her, is now in the safer, more powerful position of critic. We could conclude the daughter is failing to meet her mother's needs, but in reality she is fulfilling exactly the role needed.

A second reason children fail to meet parents' needs is that they may be incapable of it. The doctor who will settle for nothing less than a medical career for his children may have a child who loves carpentry and has little ability for medicine. The highly active boy born to parents who need a passive, conforming child is likely to be a continual source of irritation and embarrassment. He will never measure up to their expectations.

Finally, children fail to meet parents'·needs because it is impossible; no one could do it. The parents' childhood losses can never be undone; they can only be mourned. Their children can't know this, however, and assume their inability to succeed is due to a lack in themselves. They attempt with all their heart but always fall short. The parents' unhappiness and disappointment communicate that they have failed.

Thus, to one extent or another, rather than entering an environment designed to enable us to develop freely from within according to our God-given design, all of us are caught up in the tragedy of our parents' loss of their own souls. We are enslaved by emptiness and loss to which we must respond in order to survive.

TRUTH NOT BLAME

At this point you may be thinking, "Here we go again; everything is the parents' fault. Blame all the problems on them." I know many people have this image of therapy. They oppose it because they understand it as "placing the blame on your parents." And it's true that fault and blame are so much a part of our lives that it's difficult to deal with childhood pain without blaming our parents. It's also true that many people do not get beyond this point in their growth. There is some measure of

Figure 2

temporary relief in blaming our problems on others, so we can be tempted to handle them as Lucy does in figure 2.

Blaming surely doesn't solve anything, however, and we only feel better for a short time. Finding fault does not change the reality of our pain. It only shifts the guilt and shame to someone else.

That's why the process of recovery I'll describe is not based on blaming our parents. It does include facing honestly the pain we have experienced because of them. It may also include confronting them with the truth of our feelings. But it does not include blame and faultfinding.

The problems we have are true for all humanity. All of us behave in damaging ways and so hurt one another. Our parents aren't the only sources of judgment in our lives, for we have all been judged by other adults and our peers as well. Most of our pain comes from our parents, however, because we were most vulnerable to their hidden hurts and needs. They were hurt by their parents before them, too, and so on back through time to the beginning. We can only break free when we see the big picture: sin is damaging all of us.

Thus, we're caught in the pain of judgment and shame *with* our parents, not *because* of them. We must acknowledge our families are dysfunctional as part of our acceptance that "all have sinned and fall short of the glory of God" (Rom. 3:23).

Shifting the blame from child back to parent is just a revised form of the same process of judgment and shame that hurt us originally. We hurt our children in ways invisible to us, and we're helpless to prevent it. Developing new reasons for judgment and shame will not set us free; the truth sets us free.

THE FALSE SELF

How do judgment and shame affect us? They prevent the expression of who we are and trap us within ourselves. Shame becomes an automatic reaction so we cannot evaluate whether to express our feelings, desires or opinions. We become unaware of the unacceptable parts within and reveal only the acceptable. As a result, we learn to present a facade to the world instead of revealing our true selves. We hide our souls from judgment and present instead the mask to try to win attention and approval.

The child within us hides away the parts that should not be:
"I should be strong" becomes "I'm ashamed of my weakness."
"I should be nice" becomes "I'm ashamed of my anger."
"I should be submissive" becomes "I'm ashamed of my power."
"I should be brave" becomes "I'm ashamed of my fear."
"I should be dependent" becomes "I'm ashamed of my strength."
"I should be tough" becomes "I'm ashamed of my tenderness."
"I should be nonsexual" becomes "I'm ashamed of my desire."
"I should be giving" becomes "I'm ashamed of my need."

One way of representing our situation is with a diagram, like figure 3. The outer circle represents the "mask," or "false self," we learn to present, while the inner circle is the "true self" we have lost.

Most recent literature on dysfunctional families identifies the false self we develop for survival as the "codependent self." We are codependent when our dependence on other people or things results in dysfunctional behavior on our part. This includes an exaggerated concentration on the needs of others and loss of awareness of our true selves.

OUR LOST SOUL

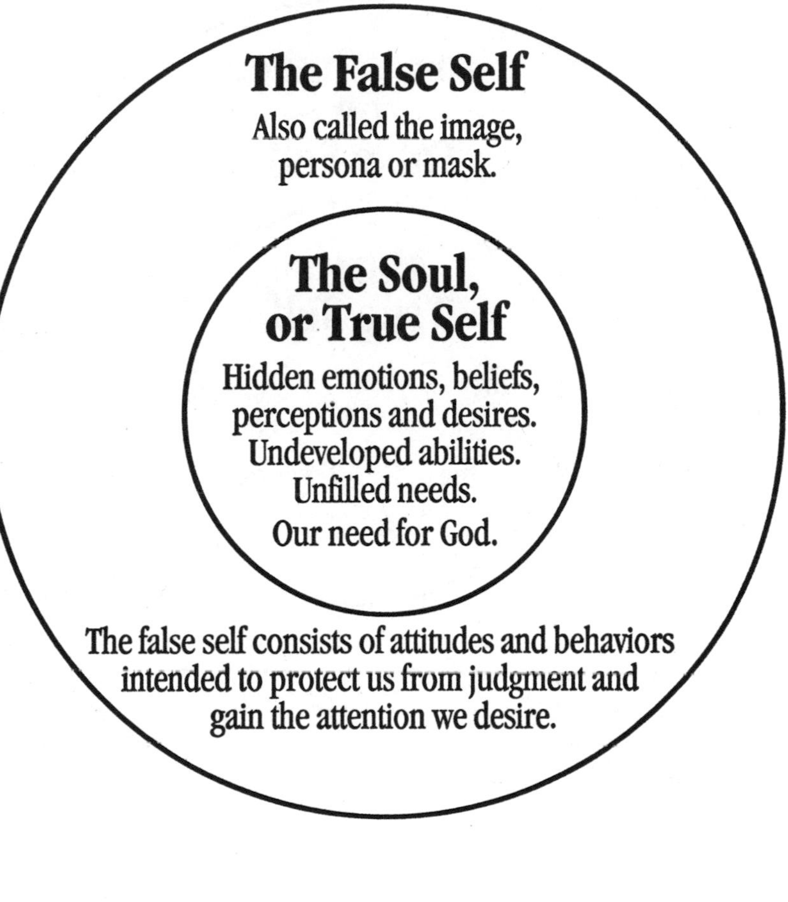

The False Self
Also called the image,
persona or mask.

The Soul, or True Self
Hidden emotions, beliefs,
perceptions and desires.
Undeveloped abilities.
Unfilled needs.
Our need for God.

The false self consists of attitudes and behaviors
intended to protect us from judgment and
gain the attention we desire.

Figure 3

MARY

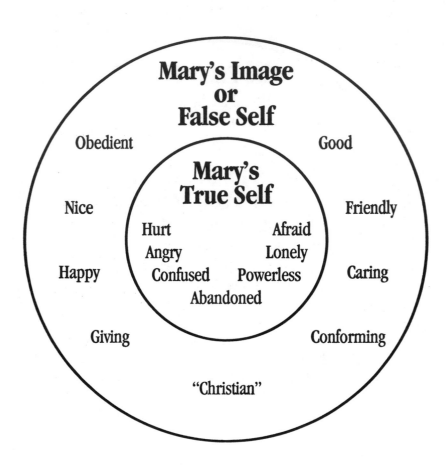

Figure 4

As we saw in Mary's case, it was not all right for her to feel her own feelings or think her own thoughts, let alone reveal them to another person. She became codependent by focusing so completely on what her parents needed her to be that she lost awareness of her true self. Her false self was competent, smiling, composed and "Christian." Her feelings of hurt, fear, anger, frustration and despair were not available to her. She had learned to present herself to the world as shown in figure 4.

Effects of Losing Our True Selves

In summary, these are some of the consequences we experience because of losing our true selves:

Physical damage. We can hold in our feelings and deny they exist, but they're never eliminated. Emotions possess power, and their power will have impact. Potential long-term physical effects include high blood pressure, ulcers and colitis.

I went years without dealing with feelings of frustration about my vocation. My blood pressure began to rise. When I finally acknowledged my feelings and dealt with them, my blood pressure dropped to a healthy level. Some researchers have even claimed to link heart disease and cancer to suppressed emotions.

Anxiety or depression. Anxiety occurs when feelings we have tried to eliminate force their way into our consciousness. We don't know their source because we have "disconnected" from our true selves. Those who cannot grieve the death of a loved one because their families say, "You should be joyful; she's now with God," will often experience anxiety. They're ashamed of their grief and are being cut off from their need to mourn. The unexpressed feelings may be experienced as anxiety.

Depression is a loss of emotional functioning and often occurs because we have no other way to deal with feelings but to "turn them off." Mary's depression came as a result of her denial of hurt, fear and unhappiness. To treat anxiety and depression, we must recover the source of our emotions and take action to care for ourselves.

Inability to feel our pain and react to it in healthy ways. We need to feel pain so we can react to it. For years, Mary had not dealt with painful situations because she didn't feel the hurt.

If someone steps on my foot, I feel pain. My natural reaction will be to cry out to express it. But if someone steps on my foot and convinces me I shouldn't hurt and I'm bad if I do, I now have two problems. The first is the pain of being stepped on; the second is how to handle the emotions I experience when the pain occurs.

If I believe I'm bad when I feel pain, I will believe I'm bad whenever I hurt. I will feel ashamed of who I am: someone who feels pain. But God created the pain system to protect us from damage. If my head aches continually, it's important that I go to a doctor to discover the cause. If I'm taught that I shouldn't have headaches, then I (1) feel ashamed that I do, (2) try to deny that I do, and (3) do nothing about dealing with the source of the pain. Eventually I may die from whatever is causing the headache.

Leprosy has been discovered to be a failure of the body's pain system. The leper feels no pain, so he engages in activities that damage him without his knowledge. He may reach into a fire to retrieve an object he dropped, unaware that he is destroying his hand. When we have been taught to feel ashamed of our pain and hide it, it's a kind of emotional leprosy. We destroy ourselves by continuing to engage in damaging behavior.

I recently read a true story about a man who had a heart attack while he was lying in bed next to his wife. He suffered with the pain for hours without saying a word. Eventually she realized something was wrong and got emergency help. It never occurred to him to tell her he was in pain! Likewise, if we've been taught to be ashamed of feelings of weakness or pain, we lose our ability to care for ourselves.

In losing our souls we may lose the joy of using our God-given abilities. Many of us have abilities we've never enjoyed because someone depreciated them when we were small. A friend recently told me she could play five different musical instruments. She was considering changing vocations, and we had been discussing her options. Not once had she mentioned her musical ability! She was somewhat surprised at my enthusiasm about it, because her family had never valued her ability but insisted she pursue something "practical" instead.

Many women don't reveal their abilities or pursue them aggressively because someone convinced them in childhood that "men won't like a strong female." The truth is that many men do not; they've been trained not to. Tragically, this robs women of their freedom to be themselves. Men, too, lose aspects of their true selves because they're supposed to be "masculine."

Destruction of relationships. If I feel hurt by something you said or did but can't feel or reveal my pain, we can't resolve it. If I can't communicate my thoughts and emotions, you can't know me and respond. We have relational leprosy. The hurt will still exist within me and affect my behavior toward you. I may withdraw to avoid further hurt or hurt you in return. I may become irritable or sarcastic, but we won't know why. Just as the pain system for an individual is crucial to personal survival, so also the pain system for a relationship must function for it to stay healthy.

Damaged ability to take responsibility. The recent sex scandals involving Christian television personalities are examples of such impaired ability. If we're raised to believe that our sexuality is bad, we hide our desires not only from the world, but also from ourselves. We're ashamed of our sexual feelings and thoughts. We can't discuss, pray about or experience our sexuality openly, so we can't learn how to handle it.

A basic principle of denial is that the parts we deny become incredibly strong and difficult to control. The harder we try to control by suppressing them, the stronger they become. You can't control something that doesn't exist.

Loss of our own sense of reality. In highly dysfunctional homes, children can be punished for simply observing an event the parents prefer to deny. The drunken parent falls out of his chair at the kitchen table. His son is frightened by this and tries to tell Mom about it. Mom goes on about her business as if nothing unusual has happened and tells the son to keep quiet. If he persists, he is spanked for being disrespectful toward his father. Repeated experiences like this make a child distrust his own senses and ability to understand. He becomes ashamed of his perceptions, for he's been taught they are wrong.

Compulsive behavior. When we have feelings, wants and needs we can't recognize, they create turmoil within. We find ways to distract our attention from our feelings so we can avoid the pain. There are as many ways of distracting ourselves as there are human activities. Some of the more common ones are eating, working, watching television, exercising, sex and talking. These are all part of a healthy life-style but can also become compulsive behaviors.

If we're compulsive, we won't be able to stop an activity without feeling anxious or agitated. When this occurs, we're no longer doing the activity for the pleasure or rewards it brings but are using it to avoid facing ourselves. Compulsivity leads to consequences of its own, such as loss of health, time, money and relationships. Many compulsive behaviors such as overeating, workaholism and "tuning out" in front of television are accepted as normal in our society.

Possible use of drugs leading to addiction. Drugs help us escape our pain or provide a few minutes of feeling good, but they have a power of their own. Addiction is a step beyond compulsive behavior, because the body develops a physical dependence. Once hooked, a person can't deal with his emotional slavery without first breaking the physical addiction. The solution to our emotional problems has then become a life-threatening problem itself, another wall in the prison of our slavery.

Losing our true selves, our souls, results in losses physically, emotionally and relationally. We lose our abilities to protect, enjoy and take responsibility for ourselves. *It creates a war within us.* When Paul stat-

> *Our internal wars are unique to each of us, but they are there. We have lost contact with parts of us that God created in order to maintain our health and enhance our joy.*

ed that he did what he hated rather than what he wanted to do (see Rom. 7:15), he revealed a problem we all experience.

The man who is ashamed of feelings of anger is an example. He constantly works not to be angry. The anger builds within until he explodes. He harms those he loves in the explosion. He feels guilty and ashamed and vows never to be angry again. Yet it builds again, he explodes again, and on and on it goes. He wants to stop the horrible cycle, but he can't. He does what he hates. He won't be able to change until he deals with the shame he feels about a God-given part of him, his anger.

Our internal wars are unique to each of us, but they are there. We have lost contact with parts of us that God created in order to maintain our health and enhance our joy.

CONCLUSION

Seeing the impact of judgment and shame in people's lives changes one's view of humanity. For me, its reality has affirmed the biblical understanding of mankind and emphasized our need for God's intervention in the cycle of our continuing self-destruction. We have all been deeply damaged, yet we've been taught not to recognize it. The Bible states that our "thinking became futile" and our "foolish hearts were darkened" (Rom. 1:21). Sin has forced us to prefer the darkness to the reality of our pain. We are not to recognize our slavery.

At one time I would have rejected this view of humanity. I would read Paul's description of our plight in the first three chapters of Romans and conclude that he wasn't talking about me or the people I knew, because his words seemed so filled with despair. I suspect many of you may be reacting to my words in a similar way. *I cannot overemphasize the reality that you cannot experience the freedom without first knowing of the slavery.* Shame and judgment destroy our relationships and ourselves. They prevent us from being the children of God we were created to be.

Jesus' invitation to become like little children and enter the kingdom of heaven is an offer of hope. We're to return to the state of vulnerability, openness and honesty we had as children. We can do this only as we're provided a way to deal with the effects of judgment and shame in our lives. Jesus has provided a way. To receive what He has provided, we must first realize our need for God.

FOR PERSONAL REFLECTION

Consider the list of emotions and traits below. Ask yourself which of these you experience and express most often. Which of these do you seldom feel or reveal to others?

Bold	Fearful
Controlling	Dependent
Strong	Weak

Sad	Joyful
Supportive	Critical
Angry	Affectionate
Aggressive	Submissive

Ask people who know you well which they see you expressing and which they seldom see from you. Was it all right for you to express these as a child? Did your parents express them? Do you allow your children to express them? Imagine yourself expressing those you don't often experience or reveal. How would you feel if you did?

All of the emotions and reactions listed above are part of being a healthy person. If you have difficulty experiencing or showing others these parts of you, you may be bound by shame in those areas of life. Consider how discovering and communicating these parts of you might help you live more fully.

FOR GROUP DISCUSSION

Role-play the following emotions with a partner.[5] Try to think of a time when you felt that emotion, and use that situation to help you "get in touch" with the feelings you're acting out. Your goal is to discover which of these emotions are difficult to express and which are not. Take your time to work through shyness or nervousness, but do take the exercise seriously. The results may be surprising.

A warning in advance: this exercise can be a lot of fun, so let yourself enjoy it. But laughter can also be a way of avoiding discomfort. For example, if you find it difficult to role-play anger without laughing or smiling, you may be discounting your anger and indicating that this emotion gives you trouble.

Strength (I'll handle———myself.) Make a fist!

Weakness (I can't do anything about————.) Slump!

Hurt (I felt really hurt when you————.) Cry?

Fear (I become very frightened when————.) Cower!

Anger (I'm very angry with you for————.) Point at the person!

Affection (I want to hug you when————.) Hug the person!

Assertiveness (I want you to————.) Sit up and make eye contact!

Submissiveness (I'll do whatever you say.)

After completing the role-playing, discuss your responses and observations. Which were relatively easy? Which were difficult? Were there any surprises?

2
OUR NEED FOR GOD

THE BEGINNINGS OF MANKIND'S SLAVERY TO SIN

How blest are those who know their need of God; the kingdom of Heaven is theirs.
—Matthew 5:3, *NEB*

T HE loss of our souls described in the first chapter occurs when we're born into a world of needy adults. Their fundamental needs were not met because their parents before them had been needy as well. Tracing this pattern of loss and pain takes us back into the history of mankind.

The questions occur: What happened that led us to experience so much unfulfilled need? Why do people ache for something more?

The biblical answer is that we're aching for the restoration of a lost relationship with God. To recover our lost souls, we must know how we became alienated from the source of everything we need.

A WORLD OF LIES

Christ said those who recognize their need of God will inherit the kingdom of heaven (see Matt. 5:3). If God is essential to life and well-being, how could we not know we need Him? Something so basic would seem obvious, but it isn't, because we live in a world of lies. Scott Peck has written, "The only power that Satan has is through human belief in its lies."[1] Jesus identified the devil as the father of lies:

"He was a murderer from the beginning, not holding to the truth, for there is no truth in him. When he lies, he speaks his native language, for he is a liar and the father of lies" (John 8:44).

The lies of evil enslave us. The first lies humanity believed came from a serpent speaking to Eve in the garden of Eden.

In the beginning, God looked at the earth and everything in it and declared it to be good (see Gen. 1:4,10,12,18,21,25,31). All of creation was in union with Him, and His goodness was revealed through it. In the beginning we were:

- created in God's image (see Gen. 1:27)
- seen by God as good (see 1:31)
- free to enjoy all of creation (see 1:26-30)
- given power over creation (see 1:28)
- provided for by God (see 1:29)
- created for love relationships (see 2:19-24)
- free to live forever (see 2:9; 3:22)
- free of shame (see 2:25)
- free to choose against God, but warned of the consequences (see 2:16-17).

Adam and Eve's power over God's creation had only one restriction: They were not to eat of the tree of the knowledge of good and evil (see Gen. 2:17). God didn't prevent their eating but warned that they would die if they did. Being created in God's image includes being free. We are even free to distrust God, to doubt Him and to rebel against Him.

The serpent accused God of lying. He said Adam and Eve would not die if they ate of the tree (see Gen. 3:4). He also implied that God was trying to keep something good from them, that He didn't have their best interests at heart (see Gen. 3:5).

He lied not only about God, but also about them, for he implied that disobeying God would be a good thing for humanity. He tempted them to live independently of God. Humanity's decision to believe those lies has alienated us from the source of life. The untruths have been passed down from generation to generation.

The most damaging thing about growing up in a dysfunctional family is believing lies about ourselves, especially about our value. The more a family is dominated by such lies, the more dysfunctional it will be. As I stated earlier, I'm convinced that all families are dysfunctional, even those that would be considered normal by human standards, because we believe lies about God and ourselves that prevent our being who we were created to be.

There are three especially powerful and damaging lies. They're seldom communicated as boldly as I'll state them here:

- **The first lie is "You do not need God."**
  This lie suggests that we can exist separately from Him and His provision and that our own resources can sustain us. This lie is contained in the serpent's words to Eve, "You will not surely die" (Gen. 3:4). We believe we can separate from God without consequences, even in the midst of our pain.

- **The second lie is "You can control your own life and destiny."**
  This implies we can be gods ourselves, setting ourselves up separately from Him and judging Him and His creation. Rather than trusting God and His creation to be good for us, this lie tempts us to decide what is good on our own.
  The first two lies combined say, "You don't need God. You can do what you desire without respect for Him or His creation."

- **The third lie is "God does not love you."**
  In the garden, the serpent subtly suggested that God does not want the best for humanity and that they should therefore do what they desired. Believing this lie destroys our trust in God and all that comes from Him. Ultimately we even distrust God's creation of us and our own value.

If God, our Creator, doesn't love us, who will?

These lies strike at the core of our humanity. God not only loves us but is the source of *all* love. He not only has our best interests in mind, but He *is* our best interest. We are not surviving on our own and cannot experience real life or love without Him.

Anything that erects a barrier between us and God destroys us.

The process of recovery includes discovering what beliefs about ourselves, life and God are not true and replacing them with beliefs based on reality. The truth sets us free because lies enslave us. Tragically, many lies are included in seemingly "Christian" beliefs and harm people who desire to know and love God.

Christianized lies include the belief that God is a coercive, hostile Father whom we have to pacify so He won't destroy us. These damaging distortions of God's Word are usually accompanied by reminders that He loves us. As a result, we may believe in His love intellectually but *feel* forsaken and unloved. The lie can keep us from enjoying His family.

To combat the lies, we must gain a clear picture of who God is and who we are. We especially need to understand the effects of our separation from Him. To do this, I find it helpful to think of us as fish out of water.

A Fish Out of Water Is a Dead Fish

Imagine a fish swimming peacefully, unaware of the grace and beauty of its movements. The water flows through its gills, and the water's life-giving oxygen is received without awareness or effort. The fish, if it's a thinking creature, will not ask whether the situation is good or bad but will simply enjoy the life that its relationship with the water brings it. You and I, if we were asked to judge the fish in the water, probably would conclude the beauty of the relationship was good.

God's creation at the beginning of Genesis was like that. God and His creatures were in relationship, His life was breathed into them, and their lives were good.

> *The process of recovery includes discovering what beliefs about ourselves, life and God are not true and replacing them with beliefs based on reality. The truth sets us free because lies enslave us.*

If one asked the fish if living in the water was good, the question would have no meaning, for living in the water is all it knows. It has no knowledge of good and evil, nothing with which to contrast it.

In the same way, Adam and Eve had no concept of good or evil before the Fall. Everything they knew was part of what God had judged as good. They had nothing with which to compare.

C. S. Lewis identified the fundamental good of being a creation of God as the "simple good."[2] This designation is to distinguish it from the "complex good" revealed in Jesus Christ that we will explore in chapter 4.

All God's creation enjoys the simple good of being created by Him and experiencing the life and value He imparts. The fish swimming gracefully through the water and experiencing its goodness represents this.

Now suppose the fish can consider jumping out of the water. Stretch your imagination a little further by imagining that the water is alive and speaks to the fish. The water says, "If you leave me, you will die."

Is the water angry with the fish? No, it just wants the fish to know reality. If it chooses to separate from the water, there will be a painful consequence; the fish will lose its life.

The fish has a mind of its own, however, and says to the water, "I don't trust you or need you. I will decide what is good for me." Then the fish jumps out.

We know what will occur. It will immediately experience the pain of being separated from the water, the pangs of death. The fish will struggle and writhe and gradually die.

Suppose we can communicate with the fish during those few minutes before death. It isn't in the nature of the water to force the fish back into it. Though available to provide everything the fish needs, the water won't force the fish to stay.

So what would you say or do? How could you address the tragedy you see occurring before you?

You might try yelling at the poor creature. "You're a bad fish! You shouldn't have jumped out of the water! You are bad, bad, bad!"

But these statements are foolish, because they miss the point. The message the fish out of water obviously needs to hear is "You are dying! You're experiencing pain because you're out of the water! Get back in and enjoy the life it brings!"[3]

Our message must focus on the experience of the fish rather than on judging its goodness or badness. It must realize its pain is due to its separation from the water, just as we must recognize that our pain and suffering are due to separation from God.

It would be equally foolish to say to a fish *in* the water, "You're a good fish. You stay in the water, so you are very good."

It makes no sense that a fish should do anything else! Thus, it isn't a question of good or bad but of identity. Fish are created to be in water, just as people are created to be with God.

DENYING OUR NEED AND PAIN

Imagine you now tell the fish that its pain is a consequence of separation from the water, *and it replies that it's feeling no pain* and everything is just fine, thank you. It's dying before your eyes, yet it refuses to acknowledge its pain. Imagine further that many such fish are struggling outside the water. They even compare themselves and try to be better than each other.

This illustration seems ludicrous, yet we people do it all the time. We deny our pain and strive to outdo one another. This is how Paul described our refusal to face the truth:

> The wrath of God is being revealed from heaven against all the godlessness and wickedness of men who suppress the truth by their wickedness, since what may be known about God is plain to them....For since the creation of the world God's invisible qualities—his eternal power and divine nature—have been clearly seen, being understood from what has been made, so that men are without excuse. For although they knew God, they neither glorified him as God nor gave thanks to him, but their thinking became futile and their foolish hearts were darkened (Rom. 1:18-21).

Our wickedness is our steadfast determination not to acknowledge our need for God or to honor Him. Karl Barth has said, "Radically and basically all sin is simply ingratitude."[4] Refusing to acknowledge God brings death, for we have broken from the Source of life.

Like the fish, people distort their thinking to believe they're doing fine even as they die. For example, when an alcoholic does this to deny his drinking, it's called alcoholic thinking. He'll twist reality by saying, "I'm not an alcoholic. I don't drink in the morning," or "I'm not an alcoholic, I don't sleep in the gutter."

Others of us tell ourselves things like these:

"I'm doing just fine. I have a good retirement saved up."

"I'm doing just fine. I have a wonderful family."

"I'm doing fine. I go to church every Sunday."

The better we thrash in death, compared to our neighbors, the harder it is for us to enter the kingdom of God. But all we're really proclaiming is "I'm dying better than you are."

Jesus said that it's harder for a rich man to enter the Kingdom of God than for a camel to go through the eye of a needle (see Matt. 19:24). He said this because the wealthy person's thrashing in death appears to be so superior. He's just more successful at appearing unaffected.

The poor have a better chance of seeing their need for God, for they're less able to believe the lie of self-sufficiency. "Blessed are you who are poor," Jesus said, "for yours is the kingdom of God....But woe to you who are rich, for you have already received your comfort. Woe to you who are well fed now, for you will go hungry" (Luke 6:20,24,25).

DEFINING GOOD AND EVIL

If this description is true of our need for God, how do good and evil enter into the picture?

If the water is our image of God, the Source of life and definition of good, then the fish could be said to be in a state of goodness while in the water.

Saying that the fish itself is good or bad is nonsense, just as it's nonsense to say any human being is good. This error in thinking is what Jesus underscored when He said, "Why do you call me good?...No one is good except God alone" (Luke 18:19).

This statement wasn't modesty on Jesus' part; He was simply speaking the truth. *Saying that the fish is in a state of goodness while in the water (God) is not a statement about its behavior but about its relationship with the water.*

While the fish is in the water, its gills, fins, eyes and movements all function according to their design. Its grace, beauty and life are part of the good, because it's where a fish is designed to be. To praise the fish for its behavior in the water because it's simply enjoying the life for which it was created would be foolish.

If the fish in the water is said to be in a state of goodness, then, in contrast, the fish *out* of the water is in a state of evil. Why? Because it's separated from the definition of good.

This statement is not about the behavior of the fish but about its situation. It's in tremendous pain. Its gills and fins are useless. Its muscles and movements are awkward and tragic, not graceful and smooth. It's dying. It's dysfunctional, for it cannot now live according to its design.

In the garden of Eden, the tree symbolized the choice facing mankind. We could choose to obey God or to disobey Him. Choosing to disobey God's command was equivalent to our fish's jumping out of the water.

Rather than trusting the good of our relationship with God, we chose to try to be gods and to determine good and evil ourselves. And because we chose against God, we now experience not only the good of being His creation, but also the evil of separation from Him.

We're dysfunctional individuals in dysfunctional families because we're alienated from the One within whom we're to function. We cannot exist for long separated from God. We're given time on this earth before we die so that we can realize our state and freely choose a restored relationship. Choosing not to restore our relationship with God is to choose death, both physically and spiritually.

All attempts to live outside of relationship with God can be classified as evil. The message of the Bible is not that we're to change our behavior outside that relationship. Jesus compared those who attempt such futile changes in behavior as whitewashed tombs (see Matt. 23:27,28). In truth, life exists only within Him (see John 3:15,16,36; 1 John 5:11-12), and nothing we do detached from Him will help us one bit.

WHAT IS GOD'S RESPONSE?

If God loves us, what can He do about this situation?

What can we do about the fish that refuses to return to the water? If the fish has free will and is responsible for its decision, we can't force it back. We can only allow it to experience its pain, confront it with the reality of its impending death and hope it'll change its mind. We must give it over to the consequences of its decisions.

Paul said that God has done this with humanity:

"Therefore God *gave them over* in the sinful desires of their hearts" (Rom. 1:24, italics mine).

"Because of this, God *gave them over* to shameful lusts" (Rom. 1:26, italics mine).

"Since they did not think it worthwhile to retain the knowledge of God, he *gave them over* to a depraved mind, to do what ought not to be done" (Rom. 1:28, italics mine).

God's wrath is not attack or accusation. He doesn't take His anger out on us like an abusive parent. Caring parents who want their children to mature will allow them to experience the consequences of their behavior in spite of their hurt and anger.

In the same way, God allows us to experience the results of our actions. He created and treats us as responsible beings. He "gives us over" to the consequences of our behavior.

This principle is stated often in the Bible. We're told we will be judged by our judgments (see Matt. 7:2) and that the measure we use will be measured out to us (see Luke 6:38). He allows us to experience our death even as He points out that we're dying, all in the hope that we will return to Him.

The only chance our fish has to be saved is by recognizing its pain and impending death, realizing its need for the water and finding some way to get back in. If it doesn't feel pain, it will never grasp the tragedy of its situation and respond. Human pain and death are likewise signs of our separation from God, and we must face them squarely.

THE LAW REVEALS OUR NEED

If the fish tells us it's doing fine in spite of its pain, how can we get it to recognize its dilemma? We could tell it how it would function in the water. We could say, "OK, if everything's fine, you ought to be able to do these things. Try them and see how you do."

For instance, we could tell the fish that it should be able to move gracefully simply by moving its fins. It may try it. If it does, it has no chance of success. We could also tell the fish to move its gills to receive life and energy, but its gills won't work outside the water.

These actions we're telling the fish to demonstrate are consistent with goodness, for they could be performed in the water. If the fish recognizes from the "law" we have given it that something is horribly wrong, the "law" has done its job, alerting the fish to its problem.

According to Paul, Hebrew law served the same function. It was to be our teacher, revealing through our inability to live it that we need a relationship with God. It, too, directs us to engage in good behavior *that is only possible within a relationship with God.*

The Law was not intended to bring salvation through our obedience to it, but rather through our recognition of our *failure* to live it.[5] Only through acknowledging this failure can we turn to our Creator through His Son and be saved.

This was Jesus' point in the Sermon on the Mount when

He said that our goodness must be better than that of the Pharisees if we're to "enter the kingdom of heaven" (Matt. 5:20). His clarifying the Law to include murderous and adulterous attitudes, as well as actions, (see Matt. 5:21-28) reveals we will never fulfill it ourselves.

A sad reality is that the fish may try to use the "law" to prove it's doing just fine as it is. Its attempt to swim outside the water would appear foolish to us, but it might be proud of its attempts to do so. The Pharisees were doing this same sort of thing with Moses' law, when Jesus, using another analogy, told them they were cleaning the outside of the cup while the inside remained filthy (see Matt. 23:25,26).

If we take biblical law seriously, especially the Sermon on the Mount, and examine ourselves honestly, we'll realize we're desperate. Maybe then we'll cry out for our Creator's love and life-giving Spirit.

THE NATURE OF A RELATIONSHIP WITH GOD

My analogy has probably raised a few questions.

You may protest that the fish should never have been given the choice to leave the water—that the price of freedom is too great.

Or you might say, "Put a net over the tank or something, for goodness' sake."

In other words, why did God give us such a tragic opportunity in the first place? Wouldn't it have been better to leave us to stroll the garden contentedly without introducing the possibility of evil and death?

In our pain, that might seem to us a better choice. But the answer lies in God's nature. He desires a loving relationship with free creatures who choose to love Him in return, not because they have to, but because they want to.

Most of us feel the same way, because, like God, we want

to be loved for ourselves. Although we might settle for the love of someone who can't choose, we really want the commitment of someone who freely wants us. God does, too—so much so that He allows us the opportunity to rebel.

You might now say, "OK, let's say I accept that God wants us to love Him truly and freely. If so, then why the big penalty if we don't? Why do we have to suffer and die if we choose not to love Him?"

Again the answer is in the nature of God.

The water is the source of life for the fish. It cannot change this fact. And just as water is necessary for life, so God is the Source of life for humanity.

Relationship with God is life; being outside that relationship is death—physical death and spiritual death. This truism describes our reality, given our nature and His. God simply *is*, and anything apart from Him eventually *isn't*.

- Apart from God, we are separated from the Source of all good and experience evil.
- Apart from God, we are separated from the Source of all life and experience death.
- Apart from God, we are separated from the One who is love, so we feel unloved and are unable to love.
- Apart from God, we are separated from the Source of all worth and value, so we experience worthlessness and shame.
- Apart from God, we are separated from the Source of our identity and have lost our true selves, our souls.
- Apart from God, we are separated from the One who alone can satisfy our deepest needs, and we experience emptiness.

Our losses in our separation from God may be summarized by saying we lost the glory given us as His creation. Paul stated that "all have sinned and fall short of the glory of God" (Rom. 3:23).

Glory denotes the "perfection of God's character, especially His righteousness." To say that God is the Father of glory is to describe Him as "the source from whom all Divine splendour and perfection proceed."[6]

The first people lost their glory as God's creation when they chose to glorify themselves. In contrast, Jesus said, "If I glorify myself, my glory means nothing" and went on to say that only glory given by the Father is meaningful (John 8:54).

Rather than turning to God and saying, "We ate from the tree You warned us about," Adam and Eve hid. Their shame revealed their need for and separation from God. So much for our attempts to glorify ourselves.

THE IMPACT OF SIN ON US ALL

Many object to the impact sin has on the innocent as being inconsistent with belief in a loving God.

When my clients face their childhood pain, they're often angry with God. They want to ask Him, "Why did You do it this way? It isn't fair! Why should we be so deeply hurt for what someone else did?"

Their circumstances are like those of a fish born outside the water complaining, "I never had a chance to experience the water. Why should I be punished because one of my ancestors jumped out?"

This objection should not be dismissed lightly. It reveals one of the most important characteristics of our relationship with God.

In dealing with this objection, we must first ask, "Is it true that all of mankind is suffering because of the first people's disobedience?"

Yes, Paul stated exactly this truth:

Just as sin entered the world through one man, and death through sin, and in this way death came to all men, because all sinned....Nevertheless, death reigned from the time of Adam to the time of Moses, even over those who did not sin by breaking a command, as did Adam (Rom. 5:12,14).

Sin entered the world with the first people and has been in control of us ever since, *even if, say, as newborns, we have not yet directly disobeyed a command of God* (see Rom. 5:14). We don't enter life in "bubbles" that protect us from the effects of others' decisions and sins.

> *God's creation is good. But we need a restored relationship with Him so we can enjoy and care for it together.*

On the contrary, we are deeply wounded by them. Though we want to protest that this circumstance shouldn't happen to us, we must remember that it has happened to *everyone*. We're in this sinful world together.

Although we have been granted individual freedom to determine our relationship with God, we experience the consequences of sin corporately. Every newspaper reveals examples of people damaged for life by irresponsible actions of others.

In union with God, however, we would share one another's burdens (see Gal. 6:2) and experience all of humanity as one. In God's eyes, the child starving in India is a part of you and me. God desires that we all care so much for that child that he not be left abandoned in his pain.

Our inability to adequately love the weak and innocent reveals how broken and divided mankind is. The innocent suffer because we were created to be bonded to one another in love. Just one person's breaking that bond destroys life for all.

When we ignore the pain of the dependent and helpless, we are also denying our own pain, for we, too, are weak and small. As long as we maintain our facade of self-sufficiency and don't recognize the helpless child in ourselves, we will not be truly sensitive to the needs of others. We must become like little children to enter the kingdom of heaven.

WE NEED A RESTORED RELATIONSHIP WITH GOD

As children we come into this world possessing the simple goodness of being God's creation. But we also inherit mankind's alienation from Him. We not only lack the ability to live our lives as God desires but are also deeply damaged by the actions of others. And most of this damage occurs when we are children, when we are most vulnerable.

Thus, we cannot be the people God intends us to be. To recover our ability to function in healthy ways we need a restored relationship with God within our own souls. We also need the healing love and affirmation of other people who are united with Him.

Jesus' warning that it would be better to have a millstone tied around one's neck and to be drowned in the bottom of the sea than to cause a little one to sin (see Matt. 18:6) was intended to alert us to the tragedy we create by trying to be gods. As we've seen, we're miserable gods. He entrusts His creation to us, and we demonstrate our failure as gods by destroying that which He gives.

We will not enjoy the world or ourselves as God's creation until we realize how profound Paul's words to Timothy are: "For everything God created is good, and nothing is to be rejected if it is received with thanksgiving, because it is consecrated by the word of God and prayer" (1 Tim. 4:4,5).

God's creation is good. But we need a restored relationship with Him so we can enjoy and care for it together. Our pain is intended to get our attention so we will reach out for that relationship.

We are masters at avoiding our pain and need, however, and part of breaking free from slavery is recognizing how we enslave ourselves. To do that we must recognize the faces of sin, a topic we'll consider next.

FOR PERSONAL REFLECTION

Consider the following statements about Christians. I am convinced they're lies about us and our relationship with God. I encourage you to consider each one, to ask if it has been your belief and, if so, to determine what effect it's had on your experience of God and life.

Probably, most of these statements have been emotional beliefs rather than intellectually held beliefs. An emotional belief is one you feel guilty about breaking even though you know it's OK to do so.

- I should not have doubts about God or the Bible.
- I should always be happy.
- I should not enjoy activities non-Christians enjoy.
- I should not feel angry.
- I should not feel sexual desire (except when I'm supposed to).
- I should want to go to church every Sunday.
- I should not have conflict with my spouse.
- I should never be depressed.
- I should always feel love for God.
- I should always feel God loves me.
- I should always feel loving toward others.
- I should never be afraid.

You may want to reword some of these to fit a particular lie that has hurt you or even add a few to the list.

FOR GROUP DISCUSSION

Do the exercise under "Personal Reflection" with special emphasis on identifying lies *you* have believed. Perhaps there are beliefs you're unsure of and would like to discuss. You may even want to point out ways you disagree with my list! Bring all these to your group for discussion.

As you gather together, make a conscious commitment to "agree to disagree." The more safety you provide for honesty, the more freedom will come in discussion. You may discover others have struggled with the same issues, and just knowing this can help.

Unless your group has a preferred format, I encourage letting people participate on a totally voluntary basis, focusing on one lie and its effects, until the group or your leader decides the topic is exhausted. Then close with prayer for God's insight and healing.

3

THREE FACES OF SIN

DENYING OUR PAIN AND NEED

*For whoever wants to save his life
will lose it....What good will it be for
a man if he gains the whole world,
yet forfeits his soul?*
—Matthew 16:25,26

I could see it coming. Roland and Jamie would start their therapy sessions smiling and in good spirits. But if anything was said to "touch a nerve," there was no stopping their race to destruction. If they weren't intercepted, Jamie would soon be in tears, and Roland would be walking out. We agreed to identify the steps they took in alienating each other so they could break their pattern.

Tonight Roland began by mentioning that Jamie had forgotten to record a check in their checkbook. His voice had a slight edge of irritation in it. Jamie picked it up from there:

> *Jamie:* You can't go one night without criticizing me, can you?
>
> *Roland:* Criticizing you? I was just telling the truth. All I said was you forgot to record the check.
>
> *Jamie:* How come the truth as you tell it is always an attack on me?
>
> *Roland:* You think everything's an attack on you. Maybe you just make a lot of mistakes.
>
> *Jamie:* There, you did it again. Ken, tell him he's attacking me.
>
> *Roland:* Leave him out of it. You're always looking for someone to be on your side. Stand up for yourself for a change.
>
> *Jamie:* So you can hit me again like you did on my birthday, you beast!
>
> *Roland:* Here we go again. That was eighteen years ago, you baby. Can't you ever forget anything? You're a real basket case, Jamie.

Jamie: (Begins to cry.) I can't forget it. You don't love me
and never have loved me.

Roland: (Interrupting.) I don't want to hear this again.

Jamie: No one has ever loved me. Everybody just picks
on me.

Roland: I do, too, love you, I really do. I just can't ever
please you.

Jamie: (Sobbing deeply.) You don't please me because you
really don't care. I wish you'd be honest and tell me
the truth.

Roland: (Reaches over to put his arms around her.) I'm
sorry, Jamie. I do love you and don't want to hurt you.

Jamie: (Abruptly stops crying.) Then why do you always
make mean remarks like about the checkbook? You
deliberately did that to hurt me.

Roland: (Defensively.) I did not try to hurt you. I never try
to hurt you. If you'd just grow up and get your act
together, we'd get along fine. It's your fault we keep
getting into these fights.

Jamie: (Bawling now.) See, you don't love me!

Roland: (Stands up.) I've had it. Women are all alike. This
is a waste of time. I'm leaving.

Jamie and Roland have not communicated. They have
unconsciously avoided real communication and left their basic
beliefs intact. Jamie's belief is "Nobody loves me." Roland's is
"All women are alike; you can't please them."

Jamie was raised in an alcoholic family with an abusive
father who rarely talked to her. Roland was raised by a needy,
irresponsible mother who expected him to be the man of the
house when his father left. As a child, he lived with the impossible burden of trying to fill a man's shoes. They're both carrying pain they have not faced and childhood losses they've not

grieved. They can't communicate honestly without facing this pain, so they repeat their ritual of destruction.

AVOIDING OUR PAIN

Roland and Jamie's difficulty in communicating is representative of problems we all have. They're trapped within false selves and childhood perceptions that prevent their hearing and responding to each other. Those false selves helped them survive childhood pain but prevent their enjoyment of marriage.

We have seen how we hide parts of our true selves in shame and present a false self to keep safe and gain acceptance. Many philosophers and theologians have written of this. Paul Tournier said, "We are the slaves of the personage which we have invented for ourselves or which has been imposed on us by others."[1] Pascal stated, "We strive continually to adorn and preserve our imaginary self, neglecting the true one."

In chapter 1 I used a diagram with two concentric circles to represent our two selves (fig. 3). The inner circle represents the true self, which includes feelings and desires we should not have, perceptions and beliefs we were taught to deny, and needs that weren't fulfilled. We hide these because we have believed one of Satan's lies, "God does not love you."

The outer circle represents the false self, the face we present to the world. This persona serves two purposes. The first is to gain acceptance and esteem to try to meet our need for love. Our belief in the lie "You don't need God" reinforces our using the false self to try to meet our needs without Him.

The second purpose the false self serves is to control people. Manipulating others to do what we want maintains our belief in the third lie, "You can be a god and control your own destiny." The barrier maintaining the false self consists of self-sufficiency (I'll meet my needs in my way) and pride (I'll control my own life).

Our false selves are also of two different types. One type we maintain through our conscious actions, the other through our unconscious, unplanned reactions. Our "public self" consists of our *actions* to create an image. We may become the "educated man," the "wealthy socialite" or the "successful career woman." We purposefully pick up the accessories to maintain these images, whether they be a college degree, a rich husband or a prestigious job. These facades are designed to make us look calm and in control and are developed in pursuit of a false god such as wealth. Goals such as education, athletic success, physical beauty or fame can bring pleasure and fulfillment, but they eventually leave us in despair if we look to them to make life worth living.

Jamie and Roland's friends only knew their "public selves." They seldom saw the hurt within them. Jamie was a successful real estate agent with an excellent reputation. Roland's career as an electrical engineer included awards for creativity. To the public, they were the ideal couple, and people were shocked when he walked out on her after nineteen years of marriage.

Our public selves may indeed function well while our relationships are falling apart. Our intimate relationships trigger our "sore points," and we react by trying to get what we need while avoiding the pain. My cool, calm, professional therapist image may disintegrate when I walk into my house and discover my children are fighting.

The false selves we use in reacting to pain do far more damage than the facades of our "public selves." They trap us within ourselves. Dr. Everett Shostrom describes this:

> People exploit, use and control each other in ways that defeat the whole purpose of their being together. The fact

is we are all manipulators—at least some of the time. We all use deceptive, insidious or unnatural devices to get the particular response we want from another person.

But how did we become manipulators? As a psychotherapist, I can explain it this way: At some point in our early development, we formed the notion that we're unacceptable as we are, that other people's opinion of how we ought to be is more important than our own opinion of ourselves.

To show people the face we think they want to see, we don a mask—the mask of manipulator....As manipulators, we refuse to allow others to be *who they are*. Instead we get stuck and stay stuck in unsatisfying relationships and lives.[2]

Being "stuck in unsatisfying relationships and lives" describes the pain of being in a dysfunctional family and trapped in our slavery to sin. We develop these defensive reactions as children, and three of them I call the "three faces of sin." They aren't faces of sin because we're bad to develop them, for we have no choice, but because they're our attempts to live in a world alienated from God. They're the prisons we inhabit in our slavery to sin. And just as we're constantly tempted to wear them, Jesus was tempted to wear them during His fast in the wilderness.

THE FACES OF SIN

Soon after Jesus' baptism by John, the Spirit led Him into the wilderness. In obedience to His Father, He was about to begin a ministry that would take Him to rejection and suffering. In preparation, He went into the desert to fast. And in the midst of His hunger and isolation, He experienced three temptations.

Each temptation offered an alternative to the pain, enticing Him to abandon His path of obedience.

We face the same temptations every day, for they are three ways of avoiding the pain of life. We don't recognize them as sin, yet they destroy our relationships and rob us of life.

The First Face

Let's set the scene by looking at Jesus' first temptation.

> Jesus, full of the Holy Spirit, returned from the Jordan and was led by the Spirit in the desert, where for forty days he was tempted by the devil. He ate nothing during those days, and at the end of them he was hungry. The devil said to him, "If you are the Son of God, tell this stone to become bread."
>
> Jesus answered, "It is written: 'Man does not live on bread alone'" (Luke 4:1-4).

Jesus was in pain, extremely hungry and weak, so this temptation struck at the heart of what He needed. He was told to escape His pain by using His power to create bread.

It's usually appropriate for us to stop our pain, for it indicates something is amiss and needs attention. But the action we take must fit the pain we're experiencing. If the pain of hunger is only telling us the body needs food, eating bread is an appropriate response. The Spirit led Jesus to His pain, however, to give Him opportunity to obey. So the question Jesus faced in this temptation was "Do I rescue Myself from My immediate need rather than remaining true to My relationship with My Father?"

Jesus responded, "Man does not live by bread alone." To rescue Himself from pain at the cost of His relationship with God would have been to set His goals above His Father's. It would have meant believing one of Satan's lies, "You do not need God." Jesus later made this point graphically:

> If your right eye causes you to sin, gouge it out and throw it away. It is better for you to lose one part of your body than for your whole body to be thrown into hell. And if your right hand causes you to sin, cut it off and throw it away. It is better for you to lose one part of your body than for your whole body to go into hell (Matt. 5:29,30).[3]

Jesus emphasized that nothing is worth saving at the cost of the soul. His words seem shocking because we don't realize how much we lose when we choose to live apart from Him. To be rescued from pain necessary to our relationship with God is not a good thing, but a tragedy.

The first temptation implies a path Jesus could have taken away from the cross. If He had used His power to wear the face of a "Rescuer," He could have given everyone material well-being. He could have bribed the people to follow, not because they wanted to know Him and worship the Father, but because they could get what they wanted.

Jesus' response pointed out that rescuing Himself or others from pain does not change our fundamental problem: our need for and separation from God. Rescuing humanity from the consequences of its destructive actions will produce no internal change. People are hungry, but rescuing only changes the symptoms without effecting a cure. Jesus' task was not to produce new conditions on earth but to bring about the existence of new people! Our pain has a holy purpose. We need it to point us to real freedom.

We need at least three kinds of pain. First, we need the pain due to our alienation from God. It is necessary to get our attention and end our denial.

Second, we need the pain we experience in working out

our relationship with God. We must be left free to "work out our salvation with fear and trembling" (see Phil. 2:12). In the movie *The Mission*, Mendoza as an act of penance for killing his brother, is carrying a load of heavy armor up a steep cliff. A well-meaning observer sees his intense pain, believes it unnecessary, and cuts the rope tying him to his burden. Mendoza has to go back down the mountain and begin again. The Rescuer has increased his pain and burden rather than helping him.

We often can't understand the way God is working in other's lives.

> *When a loving act on our part can preserve others or enable them to accomplish something they couldn't without us, our helping is an act of love rather than being a Rescuer.*

We may disagree with the paths they're taking, but we must respect them as unique creations of God and not try to fix things that aren't our responsibility. Peter tried to rescue Jesus the night He was arrested by attacking the high priest's servant. Jesus rebuked Peter by saying "Put your sword away! Shall I not drink the cup the Father has given me?" (John 18:11). We, too, must experience our pain to develop our relationship with God.

The third pain we need is that resulting from our own actions. We learn the realities of life from this pain, so it helps us to mature. If my child spends his allowance on jelly beans and then has no money for a movie, he won't learn the wise use of money if I pay his way. I must let him feel the pain of his actions so he will learn his lesson.

These are the kinds of pain we need. But you may want to protest, "Aren't we supposed to help those who are in need and pain?" Yes, we're called to love one another, which includes rescuing the vulnerable from pain they can't prevent. Some kinds of rescuing can be healthy. Later in *The Mission*, Father

Gabriel rescues Mendoza from falling to his death. This was an act of love, because it preserved him without violating who he was. When a loving act on our part can preserve others or enable them to accomplish something they couldn't without us, our helping is an act of love rather than being a Rescuer.

Whenever people step in to prevent us from feeling *necessary* pain, however, they're harming us. Trying to "fix" the pain we feel because of separation from God is only putting a Band Aid on our deepest need and robbing us of our chance for recovery.

When Abraham was directed to sacrifice his son Isaac, it was God who ended his pain at the right time and provided a ram as a substitute. Abraham's obedience had been tested, and he had faced the pain rather than rescuing himself (see Gen. 22:12-19). In the same way, Jesus refused to turn the stones to bread and rob Himself of His opportunity for obedience.

The Second Face

The devil led him up to a high place and showed him in an instant all the kingdoms of the world. And he said to him, "I will give you all their authority and splendor, for it has been given to me, and I can give it to anyone I want to. So if you worship me, it will all be yours." Jesus answered, "It is written: 'Worship the Lord your God and serve him only'" (Luke 4:5-8).

Again the temptation offered Jesus a way to avoid His pain. He could take control. Rather than remaining submissive to His Father, He could wear the face of "Controller" and rule others. If we're in control, we can order that things be different, and instead of experiencing pain, we can "dish it out."

Ruling others is the path taken by Satan. It's the way of this world. Jesus later revealed this to the disciples: "You know that those who are regarded as rulers of the Gentiles lord it over them, and their high officials exercise authority over them. Not so with you" (Mark 10:42,43). Satan tempted Jesus to follow his ways by dominating others and forcing them to take care of His needs. If Jesus did this, He would be worshiping Satan by following him and using his methods.

Again Jesus' response cut to the core of what the devil was offering. When He said "Worship the Lord your God and serve him only," Jesus was refusing to rebel against His Father. We are not to control others by deciding for them or judging them; we are to trust them to God. It is His kingdom, not yours or mine.

The Third Face

The devil led him to Jerusalem and had him stand on the highest point of the temple. "If you are the Son of God," he said, "throw yourself down from here. For it is written: 'He will command his angels concerning you to guard you carefully; they will lift you up in their hands, so that you will not strike your foot against a stone.'" Jesus answered, "It says: 'Do not put the Lord your God to the test'" (Luke 4:9-12).

The third way out of Jesus' pain was to refuse responsibility by throwing Himself off the Temple. He would be forcing the Father to rescue Him and rejecting the task He had been given. By playing the "Victim," He would be manipulating His Father.

The Victim avoids pain by looking to someone for rescue. Rather than using his God-given authority and responsibility, the Victim refuses both and appears weak and helpless. Satan was implying to Jesus, "You're special. The Father doesn't want You to be hurt. Why take responsibility and experience pain? Avoid being responsible, and He'll rescue you."

Jesus' response was to the point: "Do not put the Lord your God to the test." We are not to test God's power by avoiding our responsibilities. Refusing to wear a seat belt because "God will protect me" is an example. We've been given the ability to make healthy decisions, and God expects us to do so.

Jesus' raising of Lazarus is an example.

> Jesus, once more deeply moved, came to the tomb. It was a cave with a stone laid across the entrance. "Take away the stone," he said.
>
> "But, Lord," said Martha, the sister of the dead man, "by this time there is a bad odor, for he has been there four days."
>
> Then Jesus said, "Did I not tell you that if you believed, you would see the glory of God?"
>
> So they took away the stone. Then Jesus looked up and said, "Father, I thank you that you have heard me..." When he had said this, Jesus called in a loud voice, "Lazarus, come out!" The dead man came out, his hands and feet wrapped with strips of linen, and a cloth around his face.
>
> Jesus said to them, "Take off the grave clothes and let him go" (John 11:38-44).

Jesus didn't take away the stone, carry Lazarus out, or remove Lazarus' grave clothes. Jesus did that which no one else could do, raise the dead. Refusing to take Lazarus' grave clothes off and waiting for Jesus to do it miraculously would be ridiculous. Yet that's our reasoning when we expect God to perform tasks we can handle.

We are responsible for our choices. God will help us only when we're beyond our abilities. We can trust God, but not by refusing responsibility.

THE FACES IN ACTION

Recovery means facing our losses, taking responsibility for dealing with our pain, and reaching out for a restored relationship with God. The three faces of sin are our methods for avoiding the pain, and thus they block our recovery. To see how they work, let's examine another conflict between Jamie and Roland. At each stage of their argument, I'll identify how they're avoiding their pain.

It's Sunday morning, they're trying to leave for church, and Roland is upset. He's afraid of the embarrassment of being late to church again. His self-esteem is based on doing things right, and being less than "good" threatens him. He hides these feelings and tries to control Jamie by telling her what she should do. Rather than revealing his fears, he wears the face of the Controller.

> *Roland:* For heaven's sake, Jamie, what's taking you so long? You should have been ready an hour ago!

Jamie feels guilty, pressured, overwhelmed and inadequate. She's afraid of Roland's criticism yet resents his expectations. She avoids vulnerability, hides her feelings, and follows his lead. She shifts the blame and guilt by judging him. She, too, wears the face of Controller.

> *Jamie:* Oh, sure, you sit around reading the paper while I'm getting the kids ready and then blame me for being late. Don't blame me for your laziness, Roland. If you had helped like you should have, I would be ready.

Roland feels guilty and inadequate for not helping prepare the kids, but he resents Jamie's expecting him to. Her attack is getting to him, so he escalates his controlling.

> *Roland:* Lazy? You call me lazy after all the work I did around here yesterday? You know *!?* good and well I

did all that yard work for you. You're so ungrateful! You should be thanking me, not attacking me.

Jamie feels afraid and unloved as Roland's attack escalates. She doesn't reveal her hurt or fear but tries to regain control by attacking his public image, his role as a father and his sincerity.

Jamie: You're a great Christian role model, aren't you? You cuss like a trooper right in front of our kids. You're nothing but a hypocrite, Roland.

With each retort, they have escalated the power of their attacks. But Roland is about to deliver the crusher. He threatens to abandon Jamie.

Roland: You certainly make for a wonderful Christian wife, Jamie. Maybe I should find a wife who supports me. Then I could be a better husband.

Jamie now feels frightened and lonely but tries one last thrust as Controller, hoping guilt will keep him from leaving.

Jamie: (Begins to cry.) Sure, go ahead and threaten to leave me like you always do. Running away is always your answer.

Her attacks on Roland's image of goodness and strength are stripping away his facade. His childhood feelings of abandonment and insecurity begin to well up. His rage pours out at Jamie in an attempt to regain control and escape the pain.

Roland: Well, anyone would want to run away from such a lousy wife. You can't cook, can't keep the house halfway decent, and you're lousy in bed!

As a child, her father's criticism and dominance overwhelmed Jamie, and weakness became her only defense. She now gives up trying to win by force and unconsciously changes strategies. The face of Controller has failed her, and she shifts to the role of the Victim.

> *Jamie:* You hate me, don't you? I give up. (Throws herself on the sofa in tears.)

This is a familiar situation for Roland, for his mother's method of control was also helplessness. Roland, as the man of the house, had to provide strength for his mother and was rewarded with her adoration. He dimly realizes he's about to be manipulated, resents it, and halfheartedly tries to control it.

> *Roland:* Oh, great, here we go again. Stop it, Jamie!

Jamie deals with her feelings of guilt and inadequacy by concluding that she is incapable of success. She doesn't reveal her feelings and take responsibility for them; she claims helplessness and incompetence. She agrees with Roland's attacks.

> *Jamie:* You're right, Roland, I can't do anything right. No matter how hard I try, I can never do anything good.

This judo-like move puts Roland in an impossible situation. If he keeps attacking, he loses his "good" image, because he's attacking a defenseless "child." As he gathers his wits about him to respond to this shift, he stays with his accusations, but their force is spent and useless. The face of the Controller is failing him. He still feels resentment but welcomes the change from attacks on his strong, sufficient image.

> *Roland:* (Stands speechless for a moment, then mutters to himself.) That's for sure.

Hurt, fear and anger are flooding Jamie, but she reveals

none of them. She now uses her ultimate weapon, the hint that she'll commit suicide.

> *Jamie:* I've never been able to do anything right. It's just not worth trying anymore. I don't even deserve to be alive.

Her total helplessness and apparent vulnerability take their toll on Roland. Her suicide would destroy his image. His fear of this and need to avoid his guilt force him to tell Jamie what she wants to hear. He takes responsibility for her pain and tries to handle it himself. He doesn't reveal his fear and guilt but shifts to the face of the Rescuer. The complete contradiction between what he's about to say and what he said before is denied, for they're now moving rapidly to safety, with their pain tucked away.

> *Roland:* Aw, come on, Jamie, you know I didn't mean what I said. You're a wonderful wife!

Rather than recognizing her capabilities and strengths, the Victim looks to others to fill her need. This isn't a desire for a relationship based on equality, but a desire to be special to someone who will protect and take care of her forever. It is Jamie's deep desire for the father she never had.

> *Jamie:* Do you really mean that? I want to believe you more than anything in the world. I need you to love me so much.

Roland's security as a child came from reassuring his mother of his love, just as his security with Jamie requires him to take on the role she needs him to fill. He has to suppress the frustration and anger he feels and be her Rescuer.

Roland: You know I love you. I wouldn't be married to you if I didn't love you, would I? You're the only woman I could ever love.

Jamie: I need to hear that so much. I can't go on if you don't love me. I can't live without you. You're everything I need.

Jamie is seducing Roland by saying he can be god, can fill her every need, and is indispensable. All of us want to hear and believe this about ourselves, and Roland buys it.

Roland: Jamie, I'll never leave you. I love you just the way you are.

Roland's final words say more than he realizes. He really does "love" her "just the way she is." Only if she needs him desperately does he feel of value. Even though he resents her weakness, he has someone to take care of and protect so he can feel superior and strong. He unknowingly deceives her by implying he can be the god she needs.

They could go on like this indefinitely, locked together in unfinished pain. Neither will experience real love until they both face the pain and stop hiding behind manipulative masks. As long as they expect one another to take care of their pain, they will never know each other. They're looking for God in their partner and will always be disappointed.

The dialogue between Roland and Jamie reveals extreme behavior but is not unrealistic. If physical violence were added to their Controller roles or actual suicide attempts to Jamie's Victim persona, the dynamics would fit highly dysfunctional relationships. Most of us are far more subtle in our use of these roles. A tone of voice or a look in our eyes may send the same messages, even though our words do not. We all wear the three faces of sin.

The Karpman Triangle

The faces of sin are characteristics of dysfunctional families and exist to different degrees in every family. They're familiar to most therapists as part of the Karpman triangle.[4] The triangle consists of the three roles Jesus refused: the Controller, the Rescuer and the Victim (see fig. 5). The Controller is often called the "persecutor" or "accuser," for accusation is one of his controlling techniques.

Three Faces of Sin

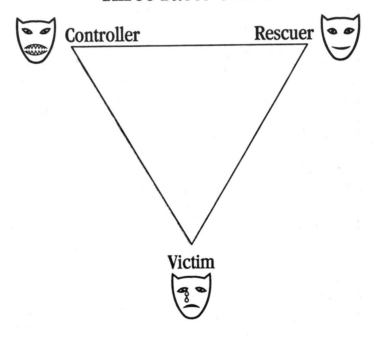

Figure 5

Dysfunctional family patterns occur when members play these roles with one another. As we saw with Jamie and Roland, people often move from one role to the next, constantly attempting to find safety and regain control. Here's another typical illustration:

Father has lost his temper and is yelling at Susie. Mother is afraid of Father's anger and steps in to rescue Susie by stopping Father. Their interchange has them in these roles:

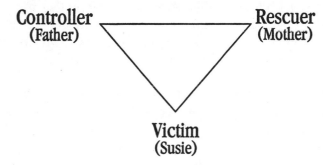

Controller
(Father)

Rescuer
(Mother)

Victim
(Susie)

In response, Father feels hurt and attacks Mother in return. Mother feels hurt and afraid but says, "You're right, I can never do anything right." Susie becomes afraid and tries to rescue Mother. Their new roles are:

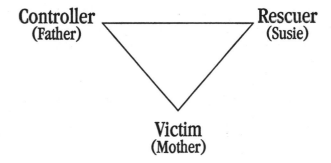

Controller
(Father)

Rescuer
(Susie)

Victim
(Mother)

Mother and Susie alternate playing Rescuer and Victim, but Father is always the Controller. Eventually he becomes the family villain and is isolated from his wife and daughter. All this occurs because each person is afraid of honestly revealing feelings.

We don't need other players to go around the triangle, however. We can do it all by ourselves. At one time I was very shy, and if I said something a little awkward in a social situation, I would attack myself within: *Ken, you dummy, that was so stupid! They think you're an idiot!* Then I would feel hurt and hopeless and think, *I can't do anything right. I give up. No one will ever like me.* Then I'd buy myself an ice cream cone to feel better.

Within a matter of minutes, I had played every role in the triangle. I wasn't facing my pain or dealing with it in a healthy way. Alcohol and other drugs are used by millions of people in similar attempts to rescue themselves from pain.

Every family and individual creates a unique variation of the triangle, but the results of playing the game are consistently tragic. No one experiences love, communication is impossible, and everyone is lonely.

In contrast, healthy relationships are based on genuine revealing of our true selves, facing pain directly, and respect for each person's integrity. Such respect means not violating others' boundaries or trying to control who they are. In doing this, we recognize ourselves and them as unique creations of God whom He loves and is working within. Healthy relationships also respect the power of each person to make decisions (exercise authority) and to handle the consequences (take responsibility). In the process, people mature. They're trusted to deal with their own pain and problems, though we may offer encouragement and support. But let's take a more-detailed look at each face of sin to see how authority and responsibility are handled dysfunctionally.

THE CONTROLLER: YOU SHOULD DO IT MY WAY

When we wear the Controller's face, we try to get what we want by playing god. We hide our pain, weakness and vulnerability and present a facade of strength, self-righteousness and intimidation (see fig. 6). We try to take away the freedom of others by creating fear or guilt within them. Controllers may be openly coercive and angry or may disguise themselves well. They may smile and say, "This is for your own

Healthy relationships are based on genuine revealing of our true selves, facing pain directly, and respect for each person's integrity.

good," while their selfish motives are hidden. They may even disguise their attacks as teasing and tell you to laugh it off, for they were "only joking." Regardless, they seem to have a knack for seeing other people's faults, just like Lucy in figure 7.

Controllers damage integrity and violate boundaries, attacking people's God-given uniqueness by telling them who they should be. They don't trust people as creations of God but judge the value of their actions and decide what's right and wrong for them. When they do this, they're trying to take God's place in a person's life *in a way God has never used*. He doesn't take away our freedom but entrusts us with it.

The motto of Controllers is "You should," which is often accompanied by "but you can't," which accuses and produces guilt. They exercise this authority over others without their consent but don't take responsibility for the results. They leave that to the Victim. As an extreme example, sexual abuse exercises authority over another's body for self-gratification, refuses to take responsibility, and abandons the victim to the consequences.

We learn to wear the face of the Controller by having it mod-

CONTROLLER

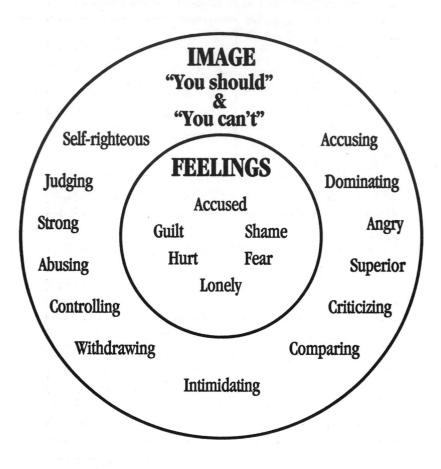

IMAGE
"You should"
&
"You can't"

Self-righteous

Accusing

Judging

Dominating

Strong

Abusing

Controlling

Withdrawing

Angry

Superior

Criticizing

Comparing

Intimidating

FEELINGS

Accused

Guilt   Shame

Hurt   Fear

Lonely

Figure 6

© 1989 United Feature Syndicate, Inc.
Reprinted by Permission

Figure 7

eled by our parents or other adults. We feel victimized by them and covet their safer position of domination. Then, when we have the chance with someone weaker, we deal with our pain by controlling or attacking. Young children become mean to the weak to deny and escape their own weakness.

Controllers say or imply, "I'm right, and you're wrong! Do it the way I say to do it!" They actually believe they're right and the world would be better if everybody did things their way. They believe in their own godliness. When we take this role, we're following Satan's model, for it is his position in accusing God and man. He challenges God's authority and strives to get us to follow his methods.

THE RESCUER: I SHOULD AND I CAN

Rescuers play god, too, but in a different way. While the Controller tries to be a god through power, Rescuers do it by being good. They allow others authority over them and then take responsibility for being who they want them to be. The motto of Rescuers is "I should and I can" (see fig. 8). They're willing to carry other's burdens, even when it's damaging to both of them. They have effectively hidden their own need and are often described as "wonderful" because they seem so caring.

At first glance, Rescuers appear to be very Christian, but it's a deception. Their goodness is not a natural outflowing of love but a facade covering a lack of feeling and life. They can't face their emptiness, so they try to be recognized and loved for doing good.

Rescuers will even create dependence in others so they'll be needed. Giving and expecting others to receive pressures them into a dependent role. The mother who insists her overweight child eat another piece of her cake is not loving him but seeking affirmation for herself. The father who insists on showering his children with gifts but doesn't require them to

RESCUER

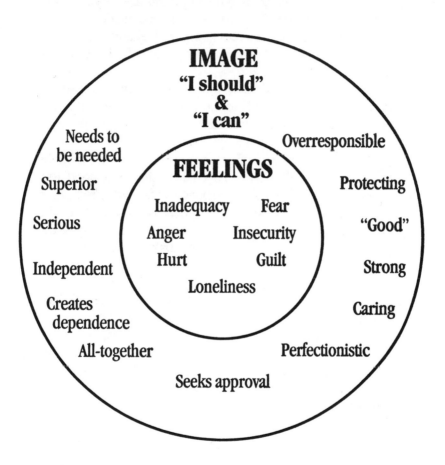

IMAGE
"I should"
&
"I can"

FEELINGS

Inadequacy   Fear

Anger   Insecurity

Hurt   Guilt

Loneliness

Needs to
be needed

Overresponsible

Superior

Protecting

Serious

"Good"

Independent

Strong

Creates
dependence

Caring

All-together

Perfectionistic

Seeks approval

Figure 8

handle money responsibly may appear loving, but he's creating dependence and weakness in them.

Like Controllers, Rescuers are at the top, or power side, of the inverted Karpman triangle. They, too, want control, but they violate others by taking away their opportunities to be responsible. Being protected from necessary pain degrades a person, yet if you refuse what Rescuers give, they feel hurt and you feel guilty. If you receive it, you feel obligated and robbed of your independence.

The Rescuer is a difficult face to recognize in ourselves, because it is so acceptable to the world. One clue is a lack of genuine emotional response. Even though we do the right things, we don't feel life and joy.

Another clue is the continual presence of guilt. Guilt can be very hard to identify, for it has been there since childhood. Rescuers feel guilty if they don't respond to another's needs, even if they know it's best not to. The spouse of the alcoholic who doesn't rescue him from the consequences of his drinking will feel guilty, even though he needs that pain desperately.

Rescuers also carry subtle feelings of superiority. "I am superior because I don't coerce or attack others" and "I am better because I have my life together and behave responsibly" are typical beliefs. This boils down to "I am superior because I am good." Occasionally someone will see through their facade and confront them as happens to Charlie Brown in figure 9. The Rescuer is trying to be god to everybody by meeting their needs, and they expect recognition for it. They can't openly seek recognition, however, because that would appear selfish. And they can't reveal their hurt and need, because then they would appear weak and fallible. So they're trapped within their own goodness and strength.

Most Rescuers were raised by parents who needed them to be good, strong and capable at an early age. The children learned they would not be loved by just being a child but could

Figure 9

avoid pain and gain approval by doing the right things. It is an especially strong role in those whose parents played the Victim. The kids had to care for the Victim parents emotionally by being sensitive and requiring little true parenting from them. Thus, the apparent goodness of adult Rescuers masks the hurt, anger and insecurity of little children who had to grow up too fast. Adults raised as Rescuers may feel they have never been children and struggle with having fun.

Other characteristics of Rescuers are:

1. Resentment at how much they're giving others.
2. Difficulty telling others no.
3. Devoting large amounts of time to things they don't want to do.
4. Experiencing emotional trauma over another person's behavior.

Rescuers appear independent, but their exaggerated focus on others' needs and neglect of their own reveal a deep dependence on others' approval. Those others continually look to them for love, because they appear so capable and caring. They themselves long for love but don't experience it, for their true selves are hidden behind an image of strength and goodness.

The Victim: I Can't, I Need You

Victims avoid their pain by manipulating someone into taking care of them. They either believe they're incapable of handling the problems of life or that they shouldn't have to. "I can't" and "I'm not responsible" are their mottos (see fig. 10).

Victims give others authority over them and then abdicate responsibility because of weakness. "You're right, I should do that, but I can't" is a frequent response. They believe they can't take actions to change or improve life, so they don't try.

VICTIM

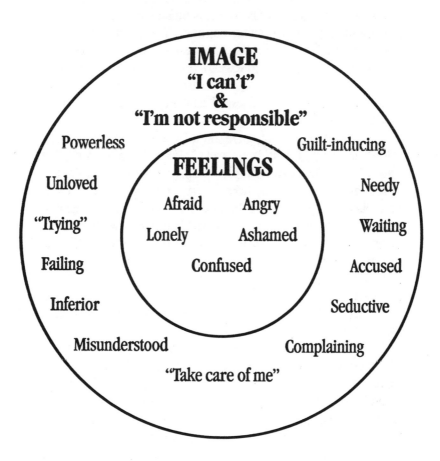

IMAGE
"I can't"
&
"I'm not responsible"

Powerless   Guilt-inducing

FEELINGS

Unloved   Needy

Afraid   Angry

"Trying"   Waiting

Lonely   Ashamed

Failing   Confused   Accused

Inferior   Seductive

Misunderstood   Complaining

"Take care of me"

Figure 10

People who play the Victim role usually had at least one parent who was a strong Controller or Rescuer. Controlling parents tell them they should and they can't, so they distrust their own strength and ability. Saying "I can't do it" gives them their only power. The classic example is the Controller parent forcefully potty-training her child. She stands over him, telling him he should "go," but nothing happens. The child has found a battle with the Controller that he doesn't have to lose. He may not win, but he can avoid loss by resisting. He holds "it" until the parent finally gives up in exasperation. Then the child walks three feet and releases "it" all over the floor, achieving a moral victory.

Victims' lives are often marked by such resistance. They don't say "I won't do it" but "I can't." "I can't have sex now; I've got a headache" is an example. "I can't mow the lawn; I'm too tired" and "I can't do my homework; they gave me too much" are also examples. Within Victims is a pattern of command—resistance. "I should mow the lawn" is the internal command, and "I can't because I'm too tired" is the resistance. Charlie Brown often plays the Victim, as he does in telling himself he shouldn't go to the movies in figure 11.

Charlie Brown never really *decides* to go to the movie and take responsibility for his decision. He resists until events catch up with him and decide his fate.

Rescuer parents create Victim children by doing everything for them and protecting them from pain. A child "forgets" to do his term paper, so the parent works all night with him to get it done. The child experiences no consequences and no growth. Another child spends all her money on video games and wants to buy a toy. The Rescuer parent gives her the money. This kind of Victim will not only believe she needs rescue, but will also demand it.

Victims need Rescuers and try to attract them. They communicate "I need you to take care of me" and "I can't live with-

© 1964 United Feature Syndicate, Inc.
Reprinted by Permission

Figure 11

out you." Rescuers are looking for people who need them so they can be recognized for how good they are. A Victim says "Here I am," and they're underway. This combination can result in marriage within days if it is intense enough. Their marriage is then based on severe need and is doomed to the kind of destructive patterns Roland and Jamie revealed earlier. The Cinderella Complex for females and the Peter Pan Syndrome for males, described in recent secular best-sellers, are entrenched Victim patterns in which people look to the opposite sex for rescue and believe themselves to be inadequate.

Victims need someone to confront them lovingly as capable creations of God and require them to face their pain and discover their strength. When this doesn't happen, the internal feelings of inadequacy and distrust of self are confirmed by others' taking care of them. Their success in manipulating robs them of self-esteem and leaves them enslaved within their mask.

A NEW FACE

Most of us use all three faces at different times, unconsciously choosing the one we believe will be most successful. The domineering man at work may walk in his front door and become his children's Rescuer. Later, in the intimacy of the bedroom, he may play the Victim to convince his wife to give him what he wants because he "can't live without it."

When I introduce the faces of sin in therapy, the most frequent question is, "What's the alternative? If I don't do these, how do I live?" Jesus revealed the answer in his response to the woman caught in adultery:

> At dawn he appeared again in the temple courts, where all the people gathered around him, and he sat down to teach them. The teachers of the law and the Pharisees brought in

a woman caught in adultery. They made her stand before the group and said to Jesus, "Teacher, this woman was caught in the act of adultery. In the Law Moses commanded us to stone such women. Now what do you say?" They were using this question as a trap, in order to have a basis for accusing him.

But Jesus bent down and started to write on the ground with his finger. When they kept on questioning him, he straightened up and said to them, "If any one of you is without sin, let him be the first to throw a stone at her." Again he stooped down and wrote on the ground.

At this, those who heard began to go away one at a time, the older ones first, until only Jesus was left, with the woman still standing there. Jesus straightened up and asked her, "Woman, where are they? Has no one condemned you?"

"No one, sir," she said.

"Then neither do I condemn you," Jesus declared. "Go now and leave your life of sin" (John 8:2-11).

If Jesus had given in to the temptation to wear one of the faces of sin in this situation, He would have become entangled in sin's trap. He refused the role of Controller by not accusing the woman or her critics. He refused the role of Victim by answering their question rather than complaining about their tactics and trying to escape. He refused the role of Rescuer by not "feeling sorry" for the woman and excusing her behavior because of the mean way she was being treated.

Jesus called everyone to responsibility. He required the accusers to look within themselves at the reality of their own sin and take responsibility for themselves rather than accusing another. He confronted the woman with the reality of her sin and encouraged her to take responsibility without excusing or condemning her. He faced reality, took responsibility, and responded in a way that required the others to do the same. Likewise, we are to use the authority God has given us and face the consequences of our own decisions and the decisions of mankind without controlling, rescuing or running away.

FACING THE CROSS

After resisting the temptations in the desert, what course was Jesus left to follow? Later in His ministry, He made this clear:

From that time on Jesus began to explain to his disciples that he must go to Jerusalem and suffer many things at the hands of the elders, chief priests and teachers of the law, and that he must be killed and on the third day be raised to life.

Peter took him aside and began to rebuke him. "Never, Lord!" he said. "This shall never happen to you!"

Jesus turned and said to Peter, "Out of my sight, Satan! You are a stumbling block to me; you do not have in mind the things of God, but the things of men" (Matt. 16:21-23).

Peter took the same role in this encounter as Satan had taken in the wilderness. He tempted Jesus to avoid His suffering and pain. Jesus' refusal to wear the three faces of sin left Him with only one choice—the cross. He decided to carry the burden of His pain and suffering faithfully in obedience to the Father. We are directed to do the same.

Then Jesus said to his disciples, "If anyone would come after me, he must deny himself and take up his cross and follow me. For whoever wants to save his life will lose it, but whoever loses his life for me will find it" (Matt. 16:24,25).

To modern minds, Jesus' instruction seems ridiculous. We

see no point in experiencing pain and avoid it at almost any cost. We spend billions of dollars on alcohol, drugs and recreation as much to avoid pain as to experience pleasure. We want to get away from ourselves. Yet Jesus calls us to face the pain and promises that if we leave our false selves, our attempts to live without God, we'll find our true selves.

We don't have to go out searching for pain; we have it in our lives already. We experience it daily and carry much of it from the past. If we avoid facing it and dealing with it responsibly, we won't grow and will not be the sons of God we were created to be. The burden for some is the pain of abuse; for others that of neglect; for some the burden of never feeling free to be themselves.

There is deep pain in all these, and it cannot be avoided without loss of life. We are called to carry our cross and follow Him. This means facing the pain and letting Him empower us to carry it. And it is in the midst of that pain and need that the tragedy, power and beauty of the Cross begin to be understood.

FOR PERSONAL REFLECTION

Explain the three faces of sin to those close to you, especially your family, and ask them which face they believe you wear most frequently. Do they say that you frequently tell them what they "should do" or get upset at them because they don't? If so, you probably spend a lot of time in the role of Controller. Parents are frequently in this role with their children. It's important to distinguish between telling children what they should do versus requiring them to become responsible. The two things are not the same.

If others report you're constantly solving problems for them or helping them, there's a good chance you're often a Rescuer, particularly if you detect irritation in them because of your help.

If others report that you frequently say you can't do what

you should be doing, can't get everything done and so on, you're probably often in the Victim role.

FOR GROUP DISCUSSION

Have four volunteers role-play members of a family attempting to solve a problem. Begin with those members who feel they "know" a particular role and can play it to help get things started. With the first group, have two volunteers play the Controller, a third the Rescuer and the last the Victim. Allow at least five minutes for the first group to play a family trying to decide what to do and where to go on vacation. Assume two of the players are the parents and the other two are teenage children. Any combination of the three roles assigned to parents and children will work. Just set them in motion and let them go.

After completing the role-play, have the observers and players share their reactions and observations with the group. What was familiar? Could you see yourself in any role? How effective was the communication achieved while playing the roles?

Try other combinations of players and roles, including some in which the players don't reveal the faces they're wearing until the play is over.

Other family problems you might use for role-playing are: Who will do which household chores, and when? Where shall we go to eat? How can we get you kids to do your homework?

In conclusion, spend a few minutes discussing this question: What do I need to help me not play roles, but to honestly reveal and take responsibility for my feelings, thoughts and desires?

PART TWO

FROM DEATH TO LIFE

4

DEATH'S POWER BROKEN

A NEW KINGDOM AND A NEW FAMILY

*He has broken the power of death
and brought life and immortality
to light through the Gospel.*
—2 Timothy 1:10 (*NEB*)

WHEN I accepted Christ as a seventeen-year-old, I hoped that becoming a Christian would end my loneliness. Those hopes were quickly squelched. The evening I first confessed my faith, the young people with me did not know how to respond. They awkwardly said they were happy for me and went their way. My loneliness remained. At first, I thought I had done something wrong, that my confession was inadequate. As I matured, I realized the freedom Christ promised was not freedom from loneliness.

We often misunderstand what it means to be free in Christ. We have our own expectations of who Christ should be and what He should do for us. When He doesn't do things our way, we get upset. People often get angry with God when I'm helping them deal with their pain. They expected Him to keep them free from suffering, and He hasn't. They've been faithful and obedient as best they could, but death, illness or divorce happened anyway. Christ has not promised us freedom from the problems and tragedies of life.

All of us want to be free of hurt, fear, and loneliness and want to be rescued from pain. Through the years, I've pursued different avenues of Christian belief, insistent on finding the freedom Christ promised. I've found that freedom now, but it's not what I expected. I was looking for freedom from pain and loneliness, instead I received the freedom to be me and the opportunity to recover my lost soul. In Jesus Christ, God has given each of us the freedom to become our true selves, to recover the persons He intends us to be.

Our recovery requires our participation and effort, and especially our honesty and courage. If we believe life will be endlessly wonderful as Christians, we'll experience disillusionment and anger. At times life *is* wonderful; at times it's very difficult. When non-Christians accuse Christians of believing so they can have a crutch, they're certainly not describing the Christian life I know. Life as a Christian is not meant to be easier, but more genuine

When we expect God to rescue us from pain because He feels sympathy for us, we're playing the Victim. If all God did was ease our pain, we would only exist, waiting to be "fixed." We would be passive, lifeless and have no value or dignity. We would only be "available" so God could show how nice He is.

This is not a biblical image of mankind or God. It turns the saga of human life into a sob story rather than a victory. God's love rescued us in a healthy way by doing what we could not, providing a way to regain our true selves. He did not play the Rescuer by taking away pain we must deal with ourselves. *The purpose of the Cross was not to ease our pain but to bring us glory.* God's intent is to create mature sons and daughters. Our response determines the life we experience.

THE MYSTERY OF CHRIST

In the first three chapters, we've explored sin and some of its consequences. Evil has broken us and left us fragmented and incomplete. We're alienated from God and dying. We're alienated from ourselves and ashamed of who we are. We're alienated from and hurt each other. Damaged people create damaged families that produce damaged children. On our own, we're helpless to do anything about it.

In the face of this tragic reality, the teachings of the Bible about Jesus Christ are astounding. According to Scripture and the testimony of millions of people, God, the source of all life and wholeness, became one of us in Jesus. His purpose was "to bring all things in heaven and on earth together under one head, even Christ" (Eph. 1:10).

Jesus Christ is the solution to all brokenness, incompleteness and division in the universe! We are reunited with God the Father *in Jesus Christ.* We are reunited inside ourselves *in Jesus Christ.* We are reunited with each other *in Jesus Christ.*

Jesus Christ is the remedy for our codependency and our dysfunctional behavior. He's so important that I would like to be able to explain Him to you. I can't. No one can. I can only point you to Him and describe what I understand and have experienced of Him. Ultimately, you must know Him for yourself. He is the mystery of the universe who brings life to all humanity, and you can be intimate with Him.

This chapter lays the foundation for the process of recovery and new life I describe in the rest of the book. That foundation is Jesus Christ. As you'll see, knowing Christ personally produces our growth, but we must first be introduced to Him and know something about who He is. Biblical truth is necessary to open our eyes. Reading this chapter may require more effort than the others; you may have to take more time to "chew" on what you read. Some of you may want to read it one time, go on to the other chapters, then return to this later.

Life in Christ as I describe it may also seem different from formulas you've learned about being a Christian. Because of this, you may have to struggle to understand and test its validity. I encourage you to take the time and put in the effort. You'll discover the gospel really is good news and is life-changing. My goal is for you to know the gift of God and experience His living water. "If you knew the gift of God and who it is that asks you for a drink, you would have asked him and he would have given you living water....Whoever drinks the water I give him will never thirst. Indeed, the water I give him will become in him a spring of water welling up to eternal life" (John 4:10,14).

Using the analogy from chapter 2, the fish can't return to the water once it has jumped out, *the water has come to the fish.* God took the initiative to come to us in Jesus and offer us living water, an inexhaustible source of life and wholeness. Because He has done that, our world is no longer the same. We now have a choice.

TWO KINGDOMS

We must choose between two kingdoms. One is a kingdom of emptiness and self-deception; the other a kingdom of life and glory. When we deny our pain and refuse to face reality, we remain in what the Bible calls "the kingdom of this world." The world is dominated by emptiness because God and His love are not trusted. In trying to fill our emptiness by controlling, competing against and manipulating others, we drain the life from them yet still remain empty.

A second kingdom, the kingdom of God, entered our world in Jesus Christ. This kingdom is filled with the glory of God, which includes His perfection, holiness, love, life, creativity and power. All that is good and gives value to life is part of God's glory and flows to everyone in His kingdom. We all hunger to be valued and loved. Our need for "self-esteem" is at heart our need for God's glory. There is no emptiness in God's kingdom, for God and His children glorify one another rather than trying to gain glory for themselves.

The world's emptiness cannot be part of God's kingdom, because its endeavors have self-glorification at heart. This kind of glory is empty. Without a change in who we are, we can't glorify one another or be part of God's kingdom, for we have nothing to offer. Emptiness can only take; it cannot give.

THE FULLNESS OF GOD IN CHRIST

In Jesus, the fullness of God entered the emptiness of the world. Love, healing and forgiveness flowed from Him. We responded by accusing, hating and crucifying Him.

Our emptiness with its resulting accusations, lies, shame and death, is alien to God and incompatible with His identity. We hate where He loves. We accuse where He forgives. We destroy where He creates. We are threatening and contradictory to God and everything in His kingdom.

His glory and our emptiness are mutually exclusive. One cannot exist in the presence of the other. Just as dryness is destroyed in the presence of water and darkness is destroyed in the presence of light, without Christ our emptiness would be destroyed in the presence of God's glory.

> *In entering our world and identifying with us, God was attacked by the power of sin and death. He identified with our weakness and vulnerability and experienced our shame and fear.*

The Bible uses the word "holy" to emphasize God's incompatibility with us. His holiness is His perfection, purity and incorruptibility. It cannot be defiled by darkness and sin. Without Jesus Christ, the division between light and darkness, goodness and evil, and life and death is total. They cannot coexist, for one is the enemy of the other. This reality is tragic for mankind, because it means there is nothing we can do to become whole.

Because of our incompatibility with God, to be human is to experience the absence of ourselves, to have been robbed of our souls by darkness and death, and then to rob others of theirs. There is no greater pain in God's universe than to lose your own identity, your very being through separation from God. It is this pain that we deny and refuse to mourn.

The mystery of Jesus Christ is that in Him, God experienced the absence of Himself. He united our emptiness with Him to provide us a way back to life. In Jesus, the great I AM experienced the total loss of all that is good, loving, beautiful and life-giving. How could God experience the absence of Himself? That is the paradox and mystery of the Cross. No words can explain it or mind fully grasp it, yet this is what was necessary for us to be reconciled with God. God's decision to become one with us in our shame and death meant that He had to experience what we do. He had never experienced shame or death, for they were alien to Him. But in Jesus, He embraced them to become one with us.

Who, being in very nature God, did not consider equality with God something to be grasped, but made himself nothing, taking the very nature of a servant, being made in human likeness. And being found in appearance as a man, he humbled himself and became obedient to death—even death on a cross! (Phil. 2:6-8).

WHAT DID CHRIST EXPERIENCE?

In entering our world and identifying with us, God was attacked by the power of sin and death. He identified with our weakness and vulnerability and experienced our shame and fear.

During the days of Jesus' life on earth, he offered up prayers and petitions with loud cries and tears to the one who could save him from death, and he was heard because of his reverent submission. Although he was a son, he learned obedience from what he suffered and, once made perfect, he became the source of eternal salvation for all who obey him (Heb. 5:7-9).

I've heard people say that Jesus could not have suffered as we do, because He knew He was God. We tragically misunderstand, however, if we believe Christ's divinity made life easier. He experienced life *more* intensely than we do, for He did not deny its pain. He obeyed in the face of His pain in the wilderness, and He even refused a painkiller while suffering on the cross.

Jesus experienced the full range of human emotions. He felt stress when people crowded and pressured Him for miracles and healings. He felt the sting of rejection in Judas's betrayal. He felt lonely and abandoned when His disciples slept in Gethsemane. He felt the grip of fear while agonizing over His decision in the garden.

By being fully God and fully human, Jesus not only revealed who God is, but He also revealed who we can be. We didn't expect His kind of divinity, however, nor did we want His kind of humanity. We anticipated a god created in our image—a controlling, dominating god. Instead, Christ revealed the God who experiences our weakness and uses His power to love, not intimidate.

> He was despised and rejected by men, a man of sorrows, and familiar with suffering. Like one from whom men hide their faces he was despised, and we esteemed him not. Surely he took up our infirmities and carried our sorrows, yet we considered him stricken by God, smitten by him, and afflicted (Isa. 53:3,4).

He "took up our infirmities and carried our sorrows" by suffering the consequences of sin for us. Jesus experienced this incredible alienation from God on the cross and cried out, "My God, my God, why have you forsaken me?" (Matt. 27:46).

The reality of this was brought home to me years ago. My family and I were attending a Christian family camp in Southern California. I had been depressed and doubting my faith for months. During the week at camp, God had set me free from the depression and communicated His love to me in specific, almost miraculous ways. At the end of the week, I knew I was free in Christ and felt more love than I had ever known.

I was not prepared for what came next, however. In the middle of our last night in camp, I awoke terrified. My family was in the room with me, but I felt totally alone. I almost screamed out in fear but seemed paralyzed. I can still see the blackness of that room, for it was the darkest black I've ever experienced. I felt totally abandoned, with no one to turn to.

> *We anticipated a god created in our image—a controlling, dominating god. Instead, Christ revealed the God who experiences our weakness and uses His power to love, not intimidate.*

As I began to ask God for help, a clear, calm message came into my mind. I didn't reason my way to it; it just appeared: "This is what I experienced for you." As I let the words sink in, I realized I was feeling a tiny portion of what Jesus had experienced on the cross. It was the most horrible emptiness I had ever known. I cried and prayed, and the feelings gradually lifted.

I awoke early the next morning and went for a walk while the sun was rising. The bright sunlight falling on the trees and flowers made me feel as if I'd been resurrected from the darkness of the night. But now I had a feeling like a deep wound within me. In one week I had become aware of both my freedom and the price paid for it. I will never forget those feelings. When I think of Christ on the cross now, His willingness to endure complete abandonment for me reveals the incredible depth of His love. He loves us more than we can know.

But he was pierced for our transgressions, he was crushed for our iniquities; the punishment that brought us peace was upon him, and by his wounds we are healed. We all, like sheep, have gone astray, each of us has turned to his own way; and the Lord has laid on him the iniquity of us all (Isa. 53:5,6).

Christ experienced the full consequences of our sin yet never turned against His Father. *By experiencing this world while remaining faithful, Christ brought God's kingdom to us.* The fullness of God prevailed in the face of all that the emptiness of evil could do.

GLORIFYING ONE ANOTHER, THE KINGDOM OF GOD

Christ not only remained obedient to the Father as the Son of God, but He also remained identified in love with you and I as the Son of Man. He entered our world, became one with us, and glorified us. *Glorifying others by revealing God's nature in them is the essence of God's kingdom.*

We can't live this way unless we know people intimately. Jesus was intimate with His Father; He was one with Him. And because He knew Him, He could glorify Him by honoring and obeying Him, thus revealing the Father's nature to us.

Satan's lies had hidden God's nature from us. By convincing us that God doesn't love us and we don't need Him, Satan had alienated us from our Father. Christ's obedience revealed a God who loves us, desires to be intimate with us, and is willing to suffer for us. Now we can recognize when the world is lying to us about God.

In response, *God glorified Jesus.* He gave Him authority and revealed His true nature to all humanity. He disclosed that Christ is His Son and is one with Him. Christ's resurrection and ascension to the Father's right hand has glorified Him for all eternity.

In the same way, *Christ glorified us by revealing our true nature.* He explained that we, too, are God's children, members of His family. Satan's accusations against us have been revealed as lies. As we glorify Christ by honoring Him as God's Son, He glorifies us as his brothers and sisters.

In bringing many sons to glory, it was fitting that God, for whom and through whom everything exists, should make the author of their salvation perfect through suffering. Both the one who makes men holy and those who are made holy are of the same family. So Jesus is not ashamed to call them brothers (Heb. 2:10,11).

Jesus glorifies us by welcoming us into a new family without shame! We have entered into God's glory. Jesus revealed this in His prayer before His crucifixion:

Father, the time has come. Glorify your Son, that your Son may glorify you....I have brought you glory on earth by completing the work you gave me to do. And now, Father, glorify me in your presence with the glory I had with you before the world began....I pray also for those who will believe in me through their message, that all of them may be one, Father, just as you are in me and I am in you. May they also be in us so that the world may believe that you have sent me. *I have given them the glory that you gave me, that they may be one as we are one* (John 17:1,4,5,20-22, itals added).

The "circle" of the giving of glory in the kingdom of God is almost complete. We provide the missing part as we do what Christ commanded: "A new commandment I give you: Love one another. As I have loved you, so you must love one another. All men will know that you are my disciples if you love one another" (John 13:34,35).

We are to love one another *as Christ loved us*. This doesn't mean we're to be "nice" or sociable but to *actually see and experience God in each other.* We are to become one in the same way Christ became one with us, by honoring each other's true nature as God's children. We are then no longer fish out of water but are reunited with our source of life. God has conquered evil and death, and as we believe and trust Christ, He conquers them in us as well.

To love and glorify Christ and each other in this way, however, we need more than the emptiness of this world from which to draw. How can we do this?

THE WORK OF THE SPIRIT

As part of the kingdom of this world, our shame, emptiness and darkness prevent us from participating in God's kingdom. Our "old self" cannot love or give, for it is empty. Paul said this old self has died in Christ.

> We died to sin; how can we live in it any longer? Or don't you know that all of us who were baptized into Christ Jesus were baptized into his death? We were therefore buried with him through baptism into death in order that, just as Christ was raised from the dead through the glory of the Father, we too may live a new life.
>
> If we have been united with him in his death, we will certainly also be united with him in his resurrection. For we know that our old self was crucified with him so that the body of sin might be rendered powerless, that we should no longer be slaves to sin—because anyone who has died has been freed from sin....In the same way, count yourselves dead to sin but alive to God in Christ Jesus (Rom. 6:2-7,11).

Since the old self is dead, we need no longer be controlled by it. We now have a new life produced by the Holy Spirit.

If you live according to the sinful nature, you will die; but if by the Spirit you put to death the misdeeds of the body, you will live, because those who are led by the Spirit of God are sons of God. For you did not receive a spirit that makes you a slave again to fear, but you received the Spirit of sonship. And by him we cry, "Abba, Father." The Spirit himself testifies with our spirit that we are God's children. Now if we are children, then we are heirs—heirs of God and co-heirs with Christ, if indeed we share in his sufferings in order that we may also share in his glory (Rom. 8:13-17).

We are no longer slaves of sin but are now sons of God, filled with the same Spirit who was in Jesus. The Holy Spirit becomes our source of love and power for living in His kingdom.

LIVING THROUGH DEATH

We enter the Christian life by dying with Christ and being resurrected a new creature. We're to *live* the Christian life in exactly the same way. C. S. Lewis said that as a result of Christ's death and resurrection, "Death itself would start working backwards."[1] Although death came because of the absence of God, now, through Jesus, it has become our way to Him. Paul said we are to be crucifying our old self and putting it to death. His words imply an active, ongoing experience of death beyond our initial identification with Christ's death in baptism.

In other words, we must work out that death in daily life. Just as we identified with the death of Christ to become Christians, so we must continue to identify with Him on the cross to crucify parts of ourselves as we become aware of them. We know from experience that our baptism into His death did not eliminate damaging behaviors or attitudes we had previously. Those elements of the world within us must die as we mature in Christ.

THE KINGDOM OF THIS WORLD

Figure 12

Christ on the cross has turned the universe right-side up. The kingdom of this world *will* become the kingdom of God. It's done, yet it's in process. I liken this to an upside-down hourglass that begins with all its sand in the bottom, representing the kingdom of this world. The top part, representing the kingdom of God, is empty in the beginning (see fig. 12). Without Christ, we're trapped in the bottom part with no way of entering God's kingdom.

Because of Christ, however, we are no longer trapped. His crucifixion and resurrection have turned the hourglass right-side-up forever. The final result is assured (see fig. 13).

Each part of the world that passes through the Cross is resurrected as a new part of God's kingdom. Just as gravity will cause all the sand in an hourglass to move to the lower part, so

THE KINGDOM OF THIS WORLD

THE KINGDOM OF GOD

Figure 13

God's grace and power will change all the world into His kingdom. In the flow of time, however, the elements of this world must pass through a little at a time.

The maturing Christian is to cooperate with God in this process. We are to give those parts of us that are part of the shame, fear and pain of this world to Jesus. We do this by opening ourselves to the light and truth of God in confession. I will illustrate this in chapter 5.

EVIL USED FOR A GREATER GOOD

As we experience resurrection, we not only recover our lost souls, but we're also given greater glory than humanity had originally. If Adam and Eve had obeyed God, they would have kept the blessings of paradise and avoided the pain of alienation from God. But Jesus Christ's obedience was far more difficult, for it was demonstrated in spite of the suffering created by sin.

I mentioned in chapter 2 that C. S. Lewis called the original good of being God's creation the "simple good." All the earth, including humanity, possesses this simple good, which evil is destroying. As Lewis pointed out, however, the good created in Jesus Christ is a goodness that God created out of the existence of evil.[2] Lewis called this the "complex good" and showed that God has used the attacks of evil to produce a greater goodness than before—a goodness even Satan cannot destroy.

> *When we face the pain of being in a sinful world and trust it to God, we're following in Christ's footsteps and turning our pain into glory.*

Satan tried to alienate Job from God by accusing him of obeying out of selfishness. He said Job didn't really love God but just wanted His rewards (see Job 1:9-11). If Adam and Eve had remained obedient, he would have accused them in the same way.

He could not accuse Christ of this, however. Jesus loved and obeyed knowing His reward would be crucifixion, not pleasure. He experienced all the suffering from Satan's attacks yet maintained the integrity of His relationship with the Father. Thus, there is no accusation Satan can bring against Christ. He can't accuse Him of having any other motivation but love for His father.

Through Christ's obedience, God used evil to create a goodness greater than would have existed if evil had not entered the world. We can demonstrate this same goodness as we become one with Christ.

God's act of grace is out of all proportion to Adam's wrong-doing. For if the wrongdoing of that one man brought death upon so many, its effect is vastly exceeded by the grace of God and the gift that came to so many by the grace of the one man, Jesus Christ....For if by the wrongdoing of that one man death established its reign, through a single sinner, much more shall those who receive in far greater measure God's grace, and his gift of righteousness, live and reign through the one man, Jesus Christ (Rom. 5:15,17, *NEB*).

"The light shines on in the dark, and the darkness has never mastered it" (John 1:5, *NEB*). That light is now "the real light which enlightens every man" (John 1:9, *NEB*). The power of evil and death has been broken and used to God's greater glory. Now, in Jesus, we can have "the knowledge of good and evil" (Gen. 2:17) and freely choose the good.

NOTHING CAN SEPARATE US

Now only our stubbornness can prevent our salvation. Shame, fear, hurt and death can no longer separate us from God, for they have been conquered. When we face the pain of being in a sinful world and trust it to God, we're following in Christ's footsteps and turning our pain into glory. We are then carrying our cross, entrusting it to Jesus and allowing Him to resurrect new life from it. Truly, *nothing can separate us from the love of God*. We need not fear anything within us, for God will use it to His glory.

For I am convinced that neither death nor life, neither angels nor demons, neither the present nor the future, nor any powers, neither height nor depth, nor anything else in all creation, will be able to separate us from the love of God that is in Christ Jesus our Lord (Rom. 8:38,39).

Christ's resurrection on Easter morning meant the universe was no longer the same. That which had been alienated from our Creator since Eden was now integrated with Him. Death and shame were resurrected as life and glory. The atonement of humanity was complete.

There is now nothing within us that is not good or cannot be turned to good. This is the freedom of being a Christian. We need fear nothing within us, for the thoughts, feelings and desires we carry are either created by God and part of the "simple good" or, if sinful and given to Jesus on the cross, will become part of the "complex good" of God's redemption.

We must know this truth to recover from the damage and power of sin. There is nothing the love of God cannot handle. If we believe this, we can face anything, including the pain of our childhoods, our families, or events that bring loss.

Christ did not end our pain on the cross; He purchased our freedom. Satan's accusations and lies need no longer enslave us, for their ability to alienate us from God has been destroyed. Because of the cross, I have someone to go to with my pain and despair, to have it resurrected as joy and hope.

We enter the world powerless and vulnerable and lose our souls to a world of emptiness and darkness. Jesus joined us in our weakness and suffered the abuse of this world while remaining faithful. He experienced the tragedy of humanity, reconciled it with God the Father, and provided us an avenue back into relationship with Him. We are to go through the suffering and pain into new life, for facing the darkness has become the door to enjoying the brightness of a new creation. Jesus Christ has indeed made death work backwards, for it is now our path to life.

FOR PERSONAL REFLECTION

1. I hoped God would rescue me from loneliness when I became a Christian. He didn't. What expectations have you had of God that have not been fulfilled? How do you feel about this?

Are there actions you could take to work responsibly to achieve the goal you hoped God would accomplish for you? In my case, I had to develop the courage to go places and do things with people even though I was afraid. Once I realized this was my responsibility and not God's, I developed the ability to do it. Some people expect God to bring them a mate but aren't willing to seek friendships with the opposite sex.

2. Until recently, the "glory of God" had little meaning for me. Those were words I'd heard often, but they had little personal relevance. I now believe it's important for us to recognize that we all hunger for God's glory. We're often willing to settle for just knowing we're of value; to imagine that we're created to experience *glory* is beyond our grasp. If this is as new to you as it was to me, do a word study of the word "glory" using a Bible and concordance. Write down what you discover, and share it with a friend. As you study, don't forget it is God's glory Christ desires for *you*.

FOR GROUP DISCUSSION

Activity #1: Follow each step, and then discuss your responses.

Identify the expectations you have had or still have of God.

Identify which expectations you have since realized were inappropriate or unrealistic and what convinced you to change.

Identify which expectations God has fulfilled and how He has done it. What has your role been in this?

Activity #2: Discuss your personal reactions to the teachings in this chapter about glorifying one another as evidence of the kingdom of God.

Have you experienced times when you were aware of God's glory? It may have been alone in prayer or in fellowship with other Christians. Describe these experiences.

5

LIVING IN THE LIGHT

CONFESSION: ENTERING GOD'S FAMILY

God is light; in him there is no darkness at all. If we claim to have fellowship with him yet walk in the darkness, we lie and do not live by the truth. But if we walk in the light, as he is in the light, we have fellowship with one another, and the blood of Jesus, his Son, purifies us from every sin.

—1 John 1:5-7

MILT believed in the Resurrection but had never experienced it. He had attended church as a child and believed its teachings, but being a Christian brought rules and guilt for him, not new life.

His wife, Georgi, asked him to see me because of his angry outbursts at their son. Milt said his wife had nothing to worry about, that he wouldn't hurt the boy, but that somebody had to punish him when he was bad. As a child, Milt had often been beaten with a belt by his father, but he insisted this was unrelated to how he was treating his son.

In spite of this, Georgi knew he carried feelings about his father's abuse. At times, after exploding at his son, he would grumble, "I hate it when I act like my father."

When I tried to talk to Milt about his father, however, his reaction was abrupt: "I don't want to talk about that. It won't do any good."

I suggested that facing his childhood feelings could help him relate to his son.

His eyes misted slightly, but his response was firm: "What's done is done."

Situations like Milt's are frustrating. I wanted him to know what he's missing. He believed in Jesus Christ but saw no connection between God's love and his daily life. He was not experiencing Him.

In such situations, these verses come to my mind: "In him was life, and that life was the light of men. The light shines in the darkness, but the darkness has not understood it....He was in the world, and though the world was made through him, the world did not recognize him. He came to that which was his own, but his own did not receive him" (John 1:4,5,10,11).

Christians, too, have difficulty recognizing Christ in their midst. Too often, we don't recognize His power, love or potential for healing our wounds because we haven't fully grasped the power of His work on the Cross. We don't realize *the Cross is both necessary and available to us every day of our lives.* To experience its healing power, we must continually open ourselves to the light.

Preferring the Darkness

Milt preferred to keep his pain in the darkness rather than open it up to the light of Christ. That refusal to face the truth about ourselves is what the Bible means in saying we prefer the darkness to the light.

The highly dysfunctional family reveals what happens when we prefer the darkness. Thoughts, feelings, perceptions and needs the family is ashamed of are never exposed. The more dysfunctional a family is, the more intensely the people insist on remaining in darkness.

When family members begin to recover from the pain and confused relationships of childhood, the rest of the family attempts to quiet them. They don't want reality exposed. They will say, "What's past is past," or deny the events or feelings the recovering people remember. They are afraid to speak openly about problems or hurts but expect each member to follow the unspoken family rule: *"Don't talk."*

Dysfunctional families also hide in the dark by suppressing feelings. Children learn that there are certain emotions their parents can't handle. The parents may not know how to deal with sexual or angry feelings, for example, so the children learn these are unacceptable and hide them. They learn the rule: "Don't feel."

The dependence and need of children must also be kept in the darkness in a dysfunctional family. The children learn their parents can't be depended on to meet their needs. They must grow up before their time. They conclude they should not burden their parents with needs they cannot fill and become ashamed of their neediness. They learn the family rule: *"Don't trust."*[1]

The rules, "Don't talk, don't feel, don't trust," reveal how dysfunctional families keep their true selves hidden. Shame causes them to prefer the darkness rather than honestly facing problems and feelings. There is little chance to mature in these families.

> *To live as Christians is to give up control and cooperate with God in the death of our old selves, through which we experience the resurrection of the new.*

Milt was likewise acting on the assumption that there was something shameful within him that shouldn't be revealed. He was judging it himself, playing god, deciding what's good and evil, not realizing he now has nothing to fear in opening himself to the light.

> May he strengthen you, in his glorious might, with ample power to meet whatever comes with fortitude, patience, and joy; and to give thanks to the Father who has made you fit to share the heritage of God's people *in the realm of light.*
>
> He *rescued us from the domain of darkness* and brought us away into the kingdom of his dear Son, in whom our release is secured and our sins forgiven....
>
> Through him God chose to reconcile the whole universe to himself, making peace through the shedding of his blood upon the cross—to reconcile *all* things, whether on earth or in heaven, through him alone (Col. 1:11-14,20, *NEB*).

Through Jesus Christ we may now live in the light, for *all things*, including anything we carry within us, have been reconciled with God. We need no longer remain in darkness, for we have been saved from it. If we continue to prefer the darkness by refusing to reveal ourselves, as Milt did, we remain empty and alone.

By trying to be strong and control life, Milt was losing it. Being strong and in control makes sense in human terms, but it's not the way of God's kingdom. Christ truly will "destroy the wisdom of the wise" (1 Cor. 1:19).

Our life, growth and freedom all occur in paradoxical ways. We gain our strength by becoming weak, achieve victory through surrender, and save our souls by giving them up. We establish control over our lives by relinquishing it, and, most mysterious of all, we become alive by dying.

To live as Christians is to give up control and cooperate with God in the death of our old selves, through which we experience the resurrection of the new. We enter and maintain our new lives through confession.

CONFESSION—THE FIRST STEP

Confession is revealing ourselves to God. It's the first step in the death of our attempts to hide, manipulate and control. It's a return to being trusting and childlike, and it's a genuine act of faith.

We start by admitting to ourselves, to others and to God that something is wrong within us. We stop denying our pain, our emotions and our helplessness. But confession is never easy, and it's often forced on us by events such as a death, divorce, job loss, depression or illness.

Consider Jim. Jim was a man's man, a fireman who was always strong and in charge and never revealed his pain. Everybody liked Jim, but nobody knew him.

He was often with people but seldom let down his guard. He confessed faith in Christ but never noticed the contradiction between his beliefs about masculinity and the manhood revealed in Jesus. Tragically (or fortunately) for Jim, a heart attack struck him down while he was fighting a fire and left him disabled.

The change was incredibly difficult. Jim could still participate in activities, but his stamina was short-lived. Weakness became his constant companion, and he hated it.

Gradually he withdrew from everyone and grew deeply depressed. His methods of gaining self-esteem and avoiding pain were gone. His facade of strength and control was broken, and he feared there was nothing underneath.

The parts of him that could be gentle or compassionate were strangers. He had learned from his father that those were not characteristics a man should have.

Fortunately, a friend insisted on maintaining contact even though Jim had cut off most relationships. Over a period of months, their friendship deepened. They discussed the kind of man Jesus was, a man who could cry and feel compassion. Jim knew these were missing in him, and as he realized this, he began to give himself permission to feel.

Gradually Jim confessed his fear, frustration and hurt. At first he tried to cover his pain with jokes, for he was ashamed of what he was discovering. But his friend stayed with him, accepted him, and encouraged his emerging freedom.

Gradually Jim returned to life. He's still macho in many of his attitudes, but he's growing. He's closer to his wife and family, and he's happier and more genuine than before his heart attack.

Jim's illness destroyed the Controller image he had developed to please his father. He couldn't be the "strong male" any longer, and because of the love of a friend, he broke free from his childhood rules.

Figure 14

Most of us must likewise become helpless and completely frustrated to give up our methods of control and open our hearts to God. Experiencing this feels very much like dying. Just ask Lucy (see fig. 14).

CONFESSION CRUCIFIES OUR OLD SELVES

Paul described our old selves accurately in Romans:

> We know that the law is spiritual; but I am unspiritual, sold as a slave to sin. I do not understand what I do. For what I want to do I do not do, but what I hate I do....I have the desire to do what is good, but I cannot carry it out....Now if I do what I do not want to do, it is no longer I who do it, but it is sin living in me that does it (Rom. 7:14,15,18,20).

What is the sin living in us that prevents us from doing good? In watching people recover and experience God's love, I have seen three aspects of our inner being that are responsible— three ways that sin works within us.

1. *The child within has been damaged by the sins of others.* The world has not met our needs, so we attempt to meet them in our own way. Our actions then manipulate and damage others. Two examples are violence and abusive sex. The vast majority of people in prison for violent crimes were physically abused as children, and most prostitutes were molested as children.
2. *The world's separation from God has left us with a void, an emptiness that a relationship with God is intended to fill.* We attempt to fill it by finding other gods such as people, activities and drugs. They fail and imprison us, because they are not God.
3. *Our determination to be in control rather than trust God*

is the foundation of all sin. If we could have all our hurts healed and our emptiness filled, we would still have the free choice to trust God or go our own way.

Our sin nature includes all these. In confession, we join Christ on the cross, allowing our old selves to be crucified with Him by uniting with Him in facing our shame, hurt and helplessness. That puts to death all three aspects of our sin nature:

First, confession opens the hurt child within us to the healing work of the Holy Spirit and the healing love of other people. This process recovers the child we were born to be.

Second, confession opens us to receiving the gift of God's Holy Spirit, who enables us to enjoy a relationship with God and fills our emptiness with His love.

Third and finally, confession is a decision to trust God rather than our own devices and manipulations, acknowledging we are *not* God. We may still choose not to trust, for God never takes away our freedom, but trusting Him fills us with His Spirit and empowers us to become our true selves.[2]

CONFESSION BEGINS OUR DIALOGUE WITH GOD

Francis of Assisi said prayer is a dialogue with God consisting of two questions: "Who are you, Lord, and who am I?" Viewing prayer this way has changed my life.

I know now that I'm in a relationship with Christ, just as I am with my wife. I must take the time to tell Him about me and to listen for His response. As I do this, I discover the truth about me and about Him.

Daring to engage in a dialogue with God by asking Francis's two questions is to challenge Satan's lies. All human suffering and death have come from believing lies about us and God. Jesus reveals the truth.

How do we carry on a dialogue with someone who is not

physically present? I can talk to my wife because she's with me, speaks to me, listens to me, and interacts with me. We can discover Christ's presence in the mystery Paul revealed to the Colossians:

> God gave me to present to you the word of God in its fullness—the mystery that has been kept hidden for ages and generations, but is now disclosed to the saints. To them God has chosen to make known among the Gentiles the glorious riches of this mystery, which is Christ in you, the hope of glory (Col. 1:25-27).

Christ is in us! I've known this for years, but I've only recently realized its power. Because of the Holy Spirit, you and I can talk to and relate personally with God in two ways. Protestants have neglected them both, preferring to live by biblical "rules" instead.

First, we can relate to Christ through meditation and prayer, trusting that *His Spirit is within us* and communicates with us.

Second and most neglected, *I can relate to Christ because He is in you! And you can relate to Christ because He is in me.*

CONFESSING TO THE SPIRIT OF GOD WITHIN

We can personally speak with God by confessing to and trusting His Spirit within us. But this presents a problem. How do we know what to trust and what to distrust? The absence of a relationship with God left us diseased within.

As Jesus said,
What comes out of a man is what makes him "unclean."
For from within, out of men's hearts, come evil thoughts,

sexual immorality, theft, murder, adultery, greed, malice, deceit, lewdness, envy, slander, arrogance and folly. All these evils come from inside and make a man "unclean" (Mark 7:20-23).

Reading verses like these and then being told to trust what's inside you seem very contradictory. To understand, we must remember that closing off our hearts to God is what alienated us from Him. The wickedness results from allowing our pain and emotions to "spoil" within, not opening them to Him.

An analogy may help you visualize this truth:

Imagine you've been weeding your yard. At the end of the day, you put the dead plants in a plastic bag and tie it closed for disposal. You forget about the bag, however, and discover it months later. The contents have been closed off from the air the entire time, and you make the mistake of opening it.

What you discover inside is horribly ugly and foul-smelling. It's rotten and of little use. But if the same plants had been tilled into a compost pile and left open to the air, they would have become a fertilizer able to bring life to other plants.

In much the same way, when our emotions and pain are closed off within us, they "rot" and lead to diseased attitudes and behaviors. We feel ashamed of the disgusting, poisonous turmoil inside and refuse to "air it out." We continue to close our hearts off and perpetuate the problem. We assume whatever emerges from within is selfish and shameful, so *we never learn to trust the Spirit God has placed within.*

By not trusting the "God who justifies the wicked" (Rom. 4:5), we keep the emptiness and ugliness inside. *We miss the point that the same light that exposes our wickedness also cleanses us of it.* Isaiah's experience of being in the presence of God illustrates this:

In the year that King Uzziah died, I saw the Lord seated on

a throne, high and exalted, and the train of his robe filled the temple. Above him were seraphs, each with six wings....And they were calling to one another:

"Holy, holy, holy is the Lord Almighty; the whole earth is full of his glory."

At the sound of their voices the doorposts and thresholds shook and the temple was filled with smoke.

"Woe to me!" I cried. "I am ruined! For I am a man of unclean lips, and I live among a people of unclean lips, and my eyes have seen the King, the Lord Almighty."

Then one of the seraphs flew to me with a live coal in his hand, which he had taken with tongs from the altar. With it he touched my mouth and said, "See, this has touched your lips; your guilt is taken away and your sin atoned for."

Then I heard the voice of the Lord saying, "Whom shall I send? And who will go for us?"

And I said, "Here am I. Send me!" (Isa. 6:1-8).

Isaiah's realization of his uncleanness was immediately followed by his cleansing. For us also, opening our true selves to God exposes our sinfulness but also brings cleansing and new life. As illustrated in the hourglass of chapter 4, trusting part of the kingdom of this world to Christ on the Cross resurrects it into the kingdom of God. The accusation and condemnation we fear *do not occur.*

Look again at Isaiah's experience. *No one accused him.* No one pointed a judging finger at him to get him to realize his uncleanness.

Isaiah felt no guilt and shame in the sense we usually do. *His value and worth were not being attacked. He saw himself clearly because he was in the presence of God.*

Being in God's presence and realizing our emptiness is so different from shame and guilt that I prefer to call it *conviction.*

Shame and guilt never bring life. God's presence and light illuminating my sin are painful but never accusing.

The conviction of the Holy Spirit brings a realization of who Christ is, His love for us and the life He gives, motivating us to glorify Him. What is not of Christ is revealed as so lifeless that we feel remorse about it.

Being in God's presence is like entering an incredibly pure, bright light revealing my dirtiness and washing me clean. His presence is so filled with the power of love that I don't want to resist Him and am immediately filled with praise and love because I realize who He is. Then I, with Isaiah, want to say, "Here am I, Lord, send me!"

As Paul summarized, "For God, who said, 'Let light shine out of darkness,' made his light shine in our hearts to give us the light of the knowledge of the glory of God in the face of Christ" (2 Cor. 4:6).

We have been encouraged to walk in the light (see 1 John 1:7), and that light is within us! The same hearts that were described as "desperately wicked" before are now the dwelling place of God! *We have been given a Spirit we can trust.*

Until we believe and act on that truth, we can't be alive. Christ's Spirit will guide us in Christ's way and give us Christ's life. This is not just intellectual truth but truth about who we are.

Deep within us all there is an amazing inner sanctuary of the soul, a holy place, a Divine Center, a speaking Voice, to which we may continually return. Eternity is at our hearts, pressing upon our time-torn lives, warming us with intimations of an astounding destiny, calling us home unto Itself. Yielding to these persuasions, gladly committing ourselves in body and soul, utterly and completely to the Light Within, is the beginning of true life. It is a dynamic center, a creative Life that presses to birth within us. It is a Light

Within which illumines the face of God and casts new shadows and new glories upon the face of men. It is a seed stirring to life if we do not choke it. It is the Shekinah of the soul, the Presence in the midst. Here is the Slumbering Christ, stirring to be awakened to become the soul we clothe in earthly form and action.[3]

Walking in the Light

Trusting our inner light, the Spirit of God, begins by confessing to Him. We must acknowledge the reality of our thoughts, feelings and attitudes and then listen for the calm, quiet voice within that reveals God's truth. That gentle voice is the voice of our spirit united with the Spirit of Christ.

Listening for that voice in the silence is extremely difficult at first. We spend most of our lives avoiding silence because we're not comfortable with ourselves. When we first try staying in silence, we become aware of a mass of confused feelings and thoughts.

We must not suppress those; we need to confess them. If we don't, we'll act separately from the Spirit. When we do that, we wear the faces of sin, for we will either control, rescue or play the Victim.

Instead, we must give them to Christ to deal with and help us understand. Then our inner turmoil won't drown out the Spirit's voice.

Whatever we do, we mustn't confuse the guilt, shame and judgment we carry inside with God's voice. The Holy Spirit does not accuse God's children; He reveals Jesus Christ to them. "For you did not receive a spirit that makes you a slave again to fear, but you received the Spirit of sonship. And by him we cry, 'Abba, Father'" (Rom. 8:15).

The Spirit's revelation of truth usually happens a little at a time. Our job is not to decide for God what He should accomplish or when, but to wait for His words within. Our only responsibility is to be honest and then listen in silence, trusting God's truth will come.

CONFESSING TO CHRIST IN ONE ANOTHER

In addition to confessing to the Spirit of Christ within us, we're also called to confess to Him in one another. "Confess your sins to each other and pray for each other so that you may be healed" (Jas. 5:16).

As a therapist, I've had a unique opportunity to experience the power of face-to-face confession. I have experienced the joy of seeing new life develop in those who confess their souls to me. As a beginning counselor, it amazed me that people often changed dramatically because I listened to and cared about them. Simply hearing people reveal their true selves *without judging or giving advice* is tremendously powerful and healing.

In listening to others' confessions, you may be led to share something with them. Be sure this is of God's Spirit and not an attempt to fix or change them. *It is not your responsibility to heal them,* and any attempt to do so will be damaging. You are not God, and if you step in as a Rescuer, you're stepping between them and God.

We've been called to love one another, not heal one another. We can cooperate with God in His healing by working to understand and identify with them in their pain and communicating our concern. We can share our insight and perspective into their pain if we're invited. If not invited, our opinions may squelch their openness, even though our intentions may be admirable.

The most precious gift we can give those who confess to us is trusting the Spirit to guide them into truth. *We are called to glorify them by seeing God in them.* When we recognize they're indwelled by the Spirit, join them in their weakness and pain, and encourage them to trust the Spirit within, we're escorting them into the kingdom of God. Believing God is in them and helping them believe it as well unleashes God's healing power in their souls.

I have also experienced this truth as the one confessing. The most significant turning points in my life have come when I've made myself vulnerable and confessed to other Christians. Experiencing Christ's love through a fellow believer somehow allows it to "sink in" differently from confessional prayer.

> *Confessing one to another is perhaps the most neglected aspect of the Christian life. I am convinced we experience little power because we confess so little weakness.*

About 10 years ago, I went through a period of depression about my faith. I couldn't accept certain doctrines that I had been told Christians had to believe. I was afraid of being judged if I revealed my inner turmoil, so I kept it hidden for months.

Eventually I confessed my feelings to a person to whom I felt the Spirit had led me. I quickly discovered he was especially sensitive and informed about the issues troubling me. He seemed specifically prepared to help me.

I received God's freedom to believe differently from other Christians in a way that seemed miraculous. I was set free.

At another time, I confessed a struggle with a moral issue that had troubled me for years. The understanding and love I experienced revealed a deep pain within that had created the struggle. I felt bathed in love, and the disturbing issue lost its power in the midst of that love. I was again set free.

The vulnerability and trust personal confession entails cannot be overestimated. We must ask for God's wisdom in deciding who to trust with our confession, for some will fail us. Unconditional love is rare, so we must be cautious. Rather than opening up everything at once, reveal yourself a little bit at a time, checking to make sure it is safe to go deeper.

Don't give up the search, however, even if it's difficult. finding the people who will lovingly hear your confession can change your life. When they respond to your brokenness with the love of Christ, the freedom from judgment allows you to bring new things into the light that had been shrouded in darkness. It floods the soul with healing and power, giving the ability to deal with something you couldn't handle before.

Confessing one to another is perhaps the most neglected aspect of the Christian life. I am convinced we experience little power because we confess so little weakness.

CONFESSION IS MORE THAN REVEALING GUILT

During most of my Christian life, I understood confession to mean telling God about the bad things I did or thought. My confessions were rather predictable. I confessed angry feelings, hurtful behavior, unacceptable sexual desires and failures.

Confessing this way produced no change, for the feelings, behaviors and failures continued. I tried to control them but failed continually. My understanding of confession was too narrow to allow God a chance to work within me.

Many Christians share that misperception of confession, which assumes we're capable of knowing the difference between good and evil on our own. We're not. To assume this is to repeat the mistake of Adam and Eve, to try to know good and evil separate from God.

As Oswald Chambers said:

God is making us spell out our own souls....The only way we can be of use to God is to let Him take us through the crooks and crannies of our own characters. It is astound-

ing how ignorant we are about ourselves! We do not know
envy when we see it, or laziness or pride....

We have to get rid of the idea that we understand ourselves, it is the last conceit to go. The only One Who understands us is God.[4]

Where we believe there is good, there may be evil. Where
we're certain there is evil, God may reveal His good. We must
distrust our own convictions about good and evil, as Manuel
learned to do.

Manuel had been raised to believe sexuality was bad. As a
teen, he agonized in guilt over his sexual desires. He confessed
his "sins" to God and kept vowing to try harder. He never considered that his sexuality might be God-given but believed it
was a demon within.

His marriage was confused and painful, for he couldn't enjoy
sex, even though it was now permissible. His negative childhood beliefs could not be so easily erased. Eventually his
depression and despair convinced him he needed help.

Fortunately, Manuel revealed his pain to a Christian friend
who was honest about his sexuality. His friend's love and acceptance, along with their open sharing and prayer, helped Manuel
realize his family's teachings were robbing him and his wife of
joy. Sexually, he began to "leave" his human family and enter
into God's, finding freedom from accusation and judgment.

It's hard to recognize evil within ourselves, because our families' definitions of good and bad dominate our consciences until
we break free of them. If my parents needed me to be nonag-
gressive, compliant and nice, those characteristics will be my
definition of *good*. I will judge aggressive people as selfish and
pushy, and people who show anger as mean and undisciplined.

As long as we don't challenge the beliefs about good and
evil absorbed from our families and our culture, we remain
ashamed of parts of ourselves that were created by God. Does

this mean that everything we learned about good and evil from our parents was wrong? Of course not. The healthier our families were functioning, the fewer untruths we learned.

My point is that we must take seriously Jesus' command, "Do not judge, or you too will be judged" (Matt. 7:1), and give up our attempts to determine good and evil separate from His Spirit. *The kingdom of God is to include freedom even from our own judgment and condemnation.* We must open our entire selves to Him so that He can "destroy our determined confidence in our own convictions."[5]

Sometimes God even has to destroy our convictions about the Bible. Our rules about goodness may be lies we learned in our families or culture, or they may be the "best rules"— the ones communicated as Hebrew law in the Old Testament. If we attempt to live by the Bible as a rule book, we won't experience the life of Christ.

Jesus told the Pharisees, "You diligently study the Scriptures because you think that by them you possess eternal life. These are the Scriptures that testify about me, yet you refuse to come to me to have life" (John 5:39,40).

For many Christians, studying the Scriptures becomes an avenue for avoiding the reality of who they are and of how desperately they need a relationship with God. Bible study is intended to point us to the One who brings life, not to be an end in itself. Life is to be lived in the Spirit, not by law.

In confessing to God, we must be willing to open up feelings we have about our families. Hurt, anger, pride and shame are especially important to admit. Remember, the feelings we hide continue to have power over us and prevent those parts of us from entering the kingdom of God.

Attitudes about family will not cease to trouble us after one time of confession, however. We can't tell God once and expect that it's all resolved. Issues that go deeply into our souls, especially from our early years, are not healed quickly.

We have to remain frank before God continually as we grieve our losses. We must also discover and confess the faces of sin we wear with our families:

If we want to blame them because of hurts or neglect, we must confess our desire to be Controllers.

If we want to maintain our good image in their eyes more than we want to be God's children, we must confess our desire to be Rescuers.

If we desire their rescuing and support more than God's, we must confess playing the Victim role.

If we don't allow the Spirit to put these aspects of our old selves to death, they will continue to haunt us.

The Spirit may also convict us of the need for responsible action to deal with difficult issues or relationships. Confession begins our relationship with God, but, as we'll see in later chapters, we won't mature without obeying what the Spirit reveals.

EMOTIONS—THE WINDOW TO OUR SOULS

Confession must come from the depths of our souls. Otherwise, it's like cleaning ourselves up on the outside, but inside remaining full of wickedness (see Luke 11:39). To bare our souls, we must reveal our emotions, because thoughts alone do not expose who and what we are.

Many couples communicate their ideas and opinions very well but are blind to their emotions. These relationships die for lack of intimacy. I can't know you and you can't know me unless we disclose our feelings.

In the same way, trying to relate to God without discovering and confessing feelings leaves our true selves hidden from the Spirit within. We can't *think* our way to God. He isn't a teacher testing our thinking; He's our lover wanting to know us!

Using the emotions list at the end of this chapter has helped my dialogue with God, especially if I'm experiencing anxiety or depression. Sitting quietly with the list and confessing my emotions to Christ penetrates my defenses and opens my soul.

My devotional time this morning illustrates this point. I forgot to pray until I began to write and realized I should practice what I preach. As I sat down to pray, a brief conflict with my wife revealed something was bothering me. But I didn't know what it was.

I begin my devotional time with the prayer, "Open my eyes, Lord," and then go slowly through the emotions list. I was feeling inadequate, fearful, guilty, critical, empty, uncaring, cold, frustrated, weak, insecure, overburdened and responsible. As I confessed these to God, I realized I had fallen into a familiar trap.

My favorite face of sin is the Rescuer, so I tend to believe everybody needs me to solve his or her problems. A person in Sunday School had described a problem yesterday morning, and my wife had mentioned one the night before. In addition, a situation at church was troubling me.

As I confessed my feelings, I realized those weren't my problems. I couldn't do anything about them if I tried. I was feeling weak, inadequate and overburdened because I was trying to be God.

When I came to the word "empty" I realized I had drifted away from trusting the Spirit. With this realization, peace returned. At about the same time, I noticed it was a beautiful morning and began to anticipate my day. I hadn't seen this until I returned to trusting the Spirit within.

There were no earthshaking changes this morning, and confession doesn't usually bring momentous realizations. My confessions today simply reminded me of who I am and opened my eyes to life where there had been only emptiness and anxiety.

I encourage you to include revealing emotions in your praying, meditating or journaling. In your time of silence and confession, share your feelings with God. Hold nothing back from Him. Do not try to reveal them and then turn them off, for that's still attempting to be God yourself. Stay open, giving Him your feelings for as long as they persist, and ask for His perspective.

CONFESSION REVEALS OUR OLD SELVES

The Rescuer facade is part of my old self that has to die for me to enjoy being God's child. Confession revealed it in my morning devotions.

At other times, I've discovered feelings of resentment, disappointment and self-pity. Those reveal a part of me that plays the Victim. I usually wear this face when I'm trying to get my wife to feel guilty because she's not meeting my needs. I'm upset that no one's taking care of me, avoiding responsibility, and expecting her to be God for me.

Her failure (or healthy refusal) to do this leaves me feeling cheated and unloved. I feel as if I just can't handle it, forgetting the strength and competence I have in Christ. As I confess my false beliefs, fear and pain, the Spirit revives me.

Sometimes I discover feelings of shame or embarrassment that reveal I believe I'm unloved and bad. Discovering these beliefs allows me to challenge them by reminding myself of God's love, forgiveness and redemption. The false beliefs lose their power and can be replaced by accurate ones.

Sometimes, however, the feelings I discover in confession don't expose my beliefs, but my needs. For example, I may discover loneliness and a desire for love. That's a need God created, and it's healthy for me to go to people and ask for their caring. This is not playing the Victim, because I'm not manipulating them, not expecting them to be God, but simply wanting their love. Honestly revealing my needs makes deepening relationships possible.

CONFESSION OPENS OUR EYES

God's response to our confession is often to reveal His perspective on a problem. He opens our eyes.

An experience my son, Mark, and I shared a few years ago revealed this truth in a way we won't forget. He had worked for weeks for the money to buy a corn snake. Yes, a snake.

When he finally had his money, he prepared a cage, purchased a snake, and brought it home. My wife and I stressed the importance of an escape-proof cage, as none of us wanted a snake crawling around our house.

After enjoying Wilbur for a while, Mark put him in his cage and left for swimming practice. I was busy preparing a Sunday School lesson, my wife was at a meeting, and our two daughters, Diane and Karen, went to bed early. After working a half hour, I took a break to look in on Wilbur.

The cage was empty! I felt panicky but managed to calm myself and began to search. Mark came home soon, and we looked desperately throughout the house for a brown-and-orange snake.

I hope you have grasped the gravity of our situation and been impressed with my calm. My son's room is two doors from where my daughters were asleep. Only his bedroom door and theirs were open. If the snake wasn't in his room, it was in theirs.

I anticipated a horrible scream at any minute as Wilbur crawled into bed with them. I considered taking a flashlight into their room, crawling around on my hands and knees, and explaining when they awoke that I was just looking for an escaped snake. I rejected that choice quickly.

I also considered the results of not finding the snake and telling them they'd have to live in a house with him. That wouldn't be pleasant. I wasn't looking forward to it either.

In addition, my wife had insisted Mark guarantee to keep the snake caged before permitting the purchase, so we were both looking forward to her return home.

Mark's frustration and pain were increasing by the minute. He had worked a long time for the snake, felt guilty for allowing it to escape, and realized all the trouble we would have if we couldn't find it. After looking a long while, we reached a point of utter exhaustion.

> *Whenever we face our pain and entrust it to God and others, we recover capabilities we had lost as part of His good creation.*

I felt so helpless, I actually thought of praying. We sat down on the floor of his room together and prayed. We didn't ask specifically for help in finding the snake, but we confessed our pain and frustration and asked for God's peace and perspective.

When I opened my eyes after praying, I "happened" to be facing Wilbur's cage. I caught a glimpse of orange. Wilbur's watering dish was hollow underneath, and a bit of orange was visible through a very small hole in its side.

Could it be true? We had struggled and searched for an hour, and now, after a prayer for perspective, my eyes immediately focused on what might be Wilbur. Mark picked up the dish, and there was Wilbur, all four feet of him, curled up in a space we couldn't believe he could fit into.

The clarity of the lesson God had given seemed breathtaking. *Nothing had changed.* Only our perspective was different, but what a difference! A situation that seemed chaotic and out of control from one perspective was peaceful and under control from another.

My example may seem trivial when compared to the trauma and suffering of life, but its lesson is valid. Change in perspective is what most prayer, including confessional prayer, is about. The lies and distortions we believe damage us and cheat us of life. Entering the light by honestly revealing ourselves to Christ opens our eyes, reveals life as God sees it, and lets us enjoy it.

An Illustration

Let's consider how Milt's opening himself to the light could bring new life. You'll recall that Milt refused to face his feelings about being abused. The child within Milt carried painful feelings because of his father's beatings:

He felt guilty because he wanted to meet his father's expectations and did not.

He felt hurt because he desired his father's affection and was attacked instead.

He felt angry because, at least to some degree, he valued and wanted to protect himself from his father.

He felt ashamed because, as a child, he automatically believed there had to be something bad about himself for his father to treat him with so little respect.

Milt was confused and not sure which contradictory feelings to trust. He felt guilty about having "caused" his father's behavior yet angry with his father for treating him unjustly. *He couldn't sort out these feelings and beliefs as long as they remained in the dark.*

His desire for his father's love and wanting to please him were part of the good God created within him, but he couldn't recover those without also experiencing his pain and guilt. Milt's ability to feel was also part of God's good creation, but he refused to trust those feelings. If he opened up and confessed his pain, he would rediscover the loving, vulnerable child within him and become capable of seeing a similar child in his own son.

By refusing to open up to the light of Christ, he chose to

play god, tried to solve the problem himself, and took the role of Controller his father had used. Milt refused to let go of his own righteousness and acknowledge the pain of being human. He was also refusing to join Christ on the Cross. And he couldn't be sensitive to his son without first becoming sensitive to the hurting child in his own soul.

What would happen if he chose to let the light of Christ into the darkness? First, it would hurt. He would feel all the emotions of the little boy. He would rediscover his vulnerability, his weakness and his desire to be loved.

But the simple goodness of God's creation of him would begin to be recovered. He would become like a child again, and that part of him would be entering the Kingdom of God.

It would take time for him to grieve the loss of his father's love and the pain of his abuse. As he opened those feelings to Christ and to others who love him, however, he would experience some of the love he lost as a child. He might experience the love of a wife who cared about him and of a son who wanted his love more than anything in the world. He would be giving them opportunity to be Christ's ministers for him, because their love would help bring healing.

As he went through his pain, he would come alive again and begin to recover his soul. The good that emerged as Milt's true self was resurrected is the greater good Christ's resurrection makes possible. If Milt faced the pain of his father's abuse, he would become more sensitive to the hurt of others and capable of loving in a way that would help others heal.

Whenever we face our pain and entrust it to God and others, we recover capabilities we had lost as part of His good creation. This new goodness has an element to it that creation wouldn't have had, however—the ability to identify with others who have been hurt in similar ways and to help them be healed as well. This redemptive good brings God's love to a world of broken and vulnerable people.

THE EFFECTS OF CONFESSION

Working through our feelings and beliefs is a lifetime process. Each experience of confession crucifies a part of our old selves and resurrects someone new.[6] We aren't always aware of how the Spirit is working or what is being accomplished but if we persist in revealing our weakness and need, He is faithful.

> The Spirit helps us in our weakness. We do not know what we ought to pray, but the Spirit himself intercedes for us with groans that words cannot express. And he who searches our hearts knows the mind of the Spirit, because the Spirit intercedes for the saints in accordance with God's will (Rom. 8:26,27).

As we cooperate in allowing God's Spirit to search our hearts, cleanse us, and intercede for us, we discover sin is losing its power in our lives. This is seldom a conscious experience but occurs outside our awareness. The Spirit bears fruit without our conscious attempt to do so.

As Oswald Chambers wrote,

> This abandon to the love of Christ is the one thing that bears fruit in the life, and it will always leave the impression of the holiness and of the power of God, never of our personal holiness.[7]

The change we undergo cannot be a source of pride, because we didn't set out to change it. We have done no striving to be good but instead have recognized and confessed our inability to change ourselves. We have received a gift from God.

As we allow the light to penetrate the heights and depths of our being, we become new people. The same Spirit who reveals our old selves and puts them to death also gives us our new identity. As we not only confess to the Spirit within but also obey Him, we move from the lifelessness of thinking we are God's children to the joy of experiencing it.

Living in the light makes life an adventure. As we're willing to go through the pain and death of honest confession, we're always discovering something fresh and exciting about who we are in Christ.

FOR PERSONAL REFLECTION

During the coming week, set aside 15 minutes to half an hour per day to use the emotions list as part of a time of prayer and confession. Begin with a brief prayer such as the one I suggested earlier: "Open my eyes, Lord."

Then, if a certain event seems troublesome, focus on it and slowly look for your emotional reactions as you go down the list. If no events come to mind, just be who you are at that moment and look for your feelings. You need not restrict yourself to those on the list; if others come to mind, write them down.

Now go back through the list and ask the Spirit to reveal to you what beliefs you carry that have led to your emotions.

Finally, confess the beliefs you've discovered, and if they're contradictory to who you are in Christ or to reality about God, ask God to change those false beliefs.

If your prayer reveals something that leaves you disturbed or puzzled, ask for guidance to either find someone to share it with or for His Spirit's help in continuing to work on it in prayer.

At the end of the week, review how this process of prayer has affected your life.

FOR GROUP DISCUSSION

Do the "Personal Reflection" activity, and when you come together, discuss your experiences, difficulties, questions and discoveries.

EMOTIONS LIST

abandoned	dependent	hysterical	put down
accepted	depressed	ignored	puzzled
adequate	deprived	immature	reasonable
affectionate	despair	impatient	rebellious
afraid	destroyed	incompetent	rejected
alienated	disappointed	incomplete	resentful
alone	discouraged	indifferent	responsible
angry	disgusted	inhibited	sad
annoyed	dissatisfied	insecure	secure
anxious	distrustful	insulted	selfish
apathetic	dominated	intimate	skeptical
apprehensive	doubtful	intimidated	small
aroused	drained	irritated	smothered
ashamed	embarrassed	jealous	sorry
attacked	empty	judged	squelched
betrayed	envious	left out	strong
bitter	exasperated	lonely	stubborn
blamed	exposed	loving	stupid
bottled up	falling apart	mean	submissive
caged	fearful	mournful	supportive
caring	foolish	nervous	suspicious
challenged	forgiving	obnoxious	sympathetic
cheated	forsaken	offended	threatened
cold	frantic	on edge	timid
competent	frustrated	open	uncertain
complaining	furious	out of control	uneasy
confused	giving	outraged	unhappy
controlled	glad	overburdened	unimportant
cooperative	gloomy	overwhelmed	used
cornered	grief	paralyzed	valued
crazy	guilty	persecuted	violated
critical	happy	pessimistic	vulnerable
deceived	hassled	pleased	warm
defeated	hate	powerless	weak
defensive	helpless	prejudged	withdrawn
deflated	humiliated	pressured	worried
degraded	hurt	pulled apart	worthless

PART THREE

BECOMING WHO WE ARE

6

INTEGRITY

THE SPIRIT WITHIN

*"Teacher," they said, "we know you
are a man of integrity and that
you teach the way of God in accor-
dance with the truth. You aren't
swayed by men, because you pay
no attention to who they are."*
—Matthew 22:16

Mᴀᴛᴛ was confused. He had been dating Vicki for three years, and she was frustrated. Twice he proposed to her and backed out. A few weeks later, he returned and continued the relationship as before. Vicki complained. "I can't trust Matt's word. He says one thing and does another." Now, two weeks from a third wedding date, he was panicking again. Vicki brought him in to see me, hoping I could get him to follow through on his word.

Two powerful people controlled Matt. His mother despised Vicki and opposed their marriage. Her criticism undermined Matt's confidence, and his desire for Vicki wilted in her presence.

But when Matt was with Vicki, he could think of no one else. Vicki was active and aggressive and knew exactly what she wanted in Matt. She decided where they would go and what they would do, and she assumed their marriage was certain. Matt's questions and concerns were quickly dismissed or answered with a certainty that ended the conversation.

Separate from his mother and Vicki, Matt was bewildered. His conversation jumped from Vicki's reasons to marry to Mother's reasons against it. He had no idea what he wanted. He feared hurting his mother's feelings but hesitated to hurt Vicki. He expected me to tell him what to do. When I said I wouldn't but would help him discover what he wanted, he was frustrated. He came for two sessions and never returned. Mother and Vicki both pressured for a decision. The wedding was canceled, but he and Vicki are dating again. Nothing has changed.

Matt is what counselors call *other-directed*. He has little awareness of his own desires and is controlled by the desires of others. He's dependent on them for self-worth and has little identity of his own. He has not developed integrity in that he cannot be true to himself or be relied upon. Like a chameleon changing colors, his pleasing facade varies according to his surroundings. He is codependent.

The codependent person's adjustment of his thoughts, feelings and behaviors to the expectations of others is not a conscious choice but a pattern begun in childhood. We're all squeezed into the mold of the world and become other-directed to some degree. But to be psychologically and spiritually healthy, we must be *inner*-directed. We must be true to ourselves. Often, however, we don't know our real selves well enough to be true to them.

Jesus was not like that. Even the Pharisees recognized Him as a "man of integrity" who was not "swayed by men." He didn't change what He said or did to curry favor with men but was true to Himself. Jesus knew who He was, where He came from and where He was going (see John 13:3). To leave codependency and develop integrity, we must know our identity as Jesus did.

GOD THE SOURCE OF INTEGRITY

God is the definition and source of all integrity. When Moses asked God what name he should use for Him, "God said to Moses, 'I am who I am.'" (Exod. 3:14). To have integrity is to speak and act in ways consistent with who we are. God cannot and does not act contrary to His identity; His actions flow from who He is. His words and deeds do not need explanation or justification; they simply are because He is.

Integrity also means being whole and complete rather than divided or double-minded. God is the source of unity and wholeness, and His work in Jesus Christ is "to bring all things in heaven and on earth together under one head, even Christ" (Eph. 1:10). The tragedy of being human is that we are not whole, not who we were created to be, and divided against ourselves.

As God defines integrity, Satan defines its absence. Satan attempts to be who he is not—God. Integrity is based on truth, and lack of integrity is based on lies. In the kingdom of this world, Satan's kingdom, nothing is as it seems. Violence and war, which seem to be signs of strength, have weakness and fear at their core.

> *To have integrity is to speak and act in ways consistent with who we are.*

Human independence and self-sufficiency have dependence and need hidden just below their surface.

The conflict between good and evil centers on our integrity. The book of Job describes in capsule form the struggle occurring between God and Satan over humanity. God said, "Have you considered my servant Job? There is no one on earth like him; he is blameless and upright, a man who fears God and shuns evil. And he still maintains his integrity" (Job 2:3). God praised and enjoyed Job's integrity, and Job enjoyed his relationship with God.

Satan cast doubt on Job's integrity by accusing him of being good so he would be rewarded. He charged him with having an ulterior motive, selfishness, rather than truly loving God. Satan's goal is likewise to attack our integrity and God's and to divide God from His creation.

In the story of Job, the author portrays the adversary [Satan] in his boldest and most radical assault on God and the godly man....When God calls up the name of Job before the accuser and testifies to the righteousness of this one on the earth—this man in whom God delights—Satan attempts with one crafty thrust both to assail God's beloved and to show up God as a fool....[He] accuses Job before God. He charges that Job's godliness is evil. The very godliness in which God takes delight is void of all integrity; it is the worst of all sins. Job's godliness is self-serving; he is righteous only because it pays. If God will only let Satan tempt Job by breaking the link between righteousness and blessing, he will expose the righteous man for the sinner he is.

It is the adversary's ultimate challenge. For if the godliness of the righteous man in whom God delights can be shown to be the worst of all sins, then a chasm of alienation stands between them that cannot be bridged. Then even redemption is unthinkable, for the godliest of men will be shown to be the most ungodly. God's whole enterprise in creation and redemption will be shown to be radically flawed, and God can only sweep it all away in awful judgment.

The accusation, once raised, cannot be removed, not even by destroying the accuser. So God lets the adversary have his way with Job...so that God and the righteous Job may be vindicated and the great accuser silenced.[1]

We are part of this great drama. Satan attacks God by assailing the integrity of mankind. Our faithfulness and trust of God even in the midst of a world of emptiness and suffering are of tremendous importance.

To maintain his integrity, his relationship with God, Job had to deal with his pain and grief, and he also had to resist the accusations of his friends and his wife's lack of support. "His wife said to him, 'Are you still holding on to your integrity? Curse God and die!'" (Job 2:9).

The human being closest to him, the one he most needed and trusted, told him to forget God and give up. Job was utterly alone and yet remained faithful. "He replied, 'You are talking like a foolish woman. Shall we accept good from God, and not trouble?'" (Job 2:10). Job was so determined to keep his integrity that he was willing to resist friends and family to the point of death:

> As surely as God lives, who has denied me justice, the Almighty, who has made me taste bitterness of soul, as long as I have life within me, the breath of God in my nostrils, my lips will not speak wickedness, and my tongue will utter no deceit. I will never admit you are in the right; till I die, I will not deny my integrity (Job 27:2-5).

Though Job later complained and behaved self-righteously, he never turned against God or became unfaithful. The integrity of his relationship with God remained. And, as Job's faithfulness and integrity defeated Satan's attempts to destroy his relationship with God, so Jesus Christ's obedience and integrity have defeated Satan for all of us.

OUR INTEGRITY IN JESUS CHRIST

Jesus made an astounding claim: "'I tell you the truth,' Jesus answered, 'before Abraham was born, I am!' At this, they picked up stones to stone him" (John 8:58). Jesus was claiming the integrity of God! He was saying He is eternal and one with the great I AM. Satan tried to destroy His oneness with God, but in the resurrection, Jesus' integrity as God's Son prevailed.

But more than His own integrity was at stake in Jesus' obedience. Our integrity was also on the line, for Jesus was united with us. While Adam and Eve's integrity had been compromised and lost, Jesus maintained His in the face of Satan's attacks, and now His integrity can be ours. In Him, we can be whole. Jesus prayed to the Father, "I have given them [those who believe] the glory that you gave me, that they may be one as we are one: I in them and you in me. May they be brought to complete unity to let the world know that you sent me and have loved them even as you have loved me" (John 17:22-23).

In praying that we "be brought to complete unity," He wasn't asking only that we be united with one another, but also that we become whole within ourselves. We need no longer be divided against and alienated from our true selves. In Jesus we can have integrity; we can experience wholeness as we put to death the old self and trust Him to resurrect the new.

THE SPIRIT IS THE SOURCE OF OUR NEW IDENTITY

We can't make ourselves whole by our own effort. God has given us our new identity by placing the Spirit of Christ within us. The Spirit determines and reveals who we are. *Having faith in Christ is not only believing and trusting who He is, but also believing who we are.* God has "sent the Spirit of his Son into our hearts" (Gal. 4:6), and as we trust and obey that Spirit, the integrity of Jesus Christ becomes our own. As God's children, we need hide from no one, for there is now nothing to hide. And as we realize we're free to simply be who we are, the division within us ceases to exist, and we become whole. We gain confidence in our new selves and become so bold as to appear naked before Him.

> We are very bold. We are not like Moses, who would put a veil over his face to keep the Israelites from gazing at it while the radiance was fading away....But whenever anyone turns to the Lord, the veil is taken away. Now the Lord is the Spirit, and where the Spirit of the Lord is, there is freedom. And we, who with unveiled faces all reflect the Lord's glory, are being transformed into his likeness with ever-increasing glory, which comes from the Lord, who is the Spirit (2 Cor. 3:12-13,16-18).

As we trust ourselves to God by bringing everything into His light, not only do our old selves die, but we are "transformed into his likeness with ever-increasing glory." We are becoming like Jesus! His wholeness becomes ours.

Christ's Spirit allows us to become inner-directed. Scripture encourages us to be open to correction and information from others, but not to be directed by them. We are to be directed by the Spirit. "If the Spirit is the source of our life, let the Spirit also direct our course" (Gal. 5:25, *NEB*). As we trust the Spirit, we will not be unhealthily dependent on others for approval and direction but will look to our true selves in making decisions. We will develop integrity, for our actions will be flowing from who we really are. *To have integrity is to trust and be true to the Spirit God has given us.*

Developing this integrity includes three things: (1) knowing and recognizing the Spirit within us; (2) erecting boundaries against the world so we can hear the Spirit; and (3) being established in the Spirit.

Knowing and Recognizing the Spirit

The first event in the ministry of Jesus was His baptism by John the Baptist. "As soon as Jesus was baptized, he went up out of the water. At that moment heaven was opened, and he saw the Spirit of God descending like a dove and lighting on him. And a voice from heaven said, 'This is my Son, whom I love; with him I am well pleased'" (Matt. 3:16,17).

The Holy Spirit identified Jesus as the Son of God and revealed God's love for and pleasure in Him. This same Spirit now gives us our identity as sons of God. A reading of Ephesians 1:3-23 reveals these truths about our new identity:

1. We have been blessed with every spiritual blessing.
2. We were chosen before the creation of the world.

3. We are *holy and blameless* in His sight!
4. We have been adopted as God's children.
5. Our sins are forgiven, and we have been redeemed (set free) by God's grace.
6. We have wisdom and understanding.
7. He has revealed the mystery of life to us: all things in heaven and on earth (including us) will be together in Christ.
8. We have been given the promised Holy Spirit as a deposit guaranteeing our inheritance—final and complete redemption (freedom from sin).
9. We can know God through the Holy Spirit.
10. We have incomparably great power.

Those are the blessings the Holy Spirit brings. *Any voice within us that contradicts these realities is not the Spirit of God.* Messages producing guilt, shame and fear are in opposition to these and should be distrusted, for they are lies! They result from Satan's and humanity's accusations.

The Holy Spirit is our inner guide to being our true selves. The only guilt He brings is the deep remorse we feel when we haven't been true to our new identity. This intrinsic guilt is the conviction we feel when we enter God's light and realize the contradiction between who we are and how we're living. It is God's call to return to living as the new creatures we are.

As we trust in our new identity, our emptiness is filled. Our psychological needs of worth, belonging and competence are met in Christ. These are the needs we have hungered to have satisfied since we were born.

Worth. We need to know we are of value—that our existence is significant. God's gift of His Son communicates our eternal worth. "God so loved the world that he gave his one and only Son, that whoever believes in him shall not perish but have eternal life" (John 3:16).

Belonging. We need to know we belong to someone who desires relationship with us. We *do* belong. We have been adopted by God the Father as His children. We have left the dysfunctional human family and are now in God's. "The Spirit himself testifies with our spirit that we are God's children" (Rom. 8:16).

Competence. We need to know our existence has purpose. We need to be capable of significant accomplishments. The Spirit of Christ gives us such competence. "For God hath not given us the spirit of fear; but of power, and of love, and of a sound mind" (2 Tim. 1:7, *KJV*).[2]

After trying unsuccessfully to manipulate people to fill our needs, having them filled in Christ can affect us the way an unexpected shower affected Snoopy (see fig. 15).

As Snoopy looked to the faucet to fill his thirst, we begin our lives looking to others to fill our needs. We can never stray far from them, because we hope they will be God to us. Human sources do fill our needs in small amounts, but eventually they give us little more than a drop in our water dish and leave us still thirsty.

Jesus said, "If a man is thirsty, let him come to me and drink. Whoever believes in me, as the Scripture has said, streams of living water will flow from within him" (John 7:37,38). Just as Snoopy's thirst was filled from an unexpected source, so also is ours as God places His kingdom within us. Snoopy was hesitant to accept his full bowl. Our reactions to the good news of who we are in Christ are similar. The news is so good that it takes us a lifetime to "think about it."

WHOM DO WE TRUST?

Unfortunately, when I "think about it," my thoughts often are not positive. I read the descriptions of who I am in Christ and react with disbelief: *Who, me? I can't even go through one day*

Figure 15

without saying or doing something wrong. My thoughts are seldom "spiritual" and would be embarrassing to reveal.

At other times, I distrust my sonship because I fear a hidden price tag. *If I do believe, what do I have to do? Do I have to sell everything I've got and live in the streets? God couldn't love me so much that He would set me totally free. It's too hard to believe.*

Do you recognize the refrain? Satan still tries to rob us of our identity with his lies. He doesn't want us to experience God's love, freedom and life. *Satan doesn't want us to know that we are whole in Christ and can live confidently, knowing God is faithful and will preserve us.* He wants us to live in doubt, trying to be good, striving to do things right, but uncertain of God's love and our freedom. He prefers that we hide in the dark, refusing to trust God's love, and miss the joy of being God's children.

DISTINGUISHING OUR OLD SELVES FROM THE SPIRIT

To have integrity, we must distinguish between the truth of the Spirit and the lies that damage us. We saw in chapter 5 that God's Spirit does not accuse or condemn but convicts and cleanses. He doesn't alienate or abandon us but draws us close to God and communicates His love. *We can recognize the Spirit of God by the fruit He bears and the life He brings (see fig. 16).* *"But the fruit of the Spirit is love, joy, peace, patience, kindness, goodness, faithfulness, gentleness and self-control"* (Gal. 5:22-23). "For the letter kills, but the Spirit gives life" (2 Cor. 3:6).

The Holy Spirit points us to Christ and reveals Christ in us. We can recognize His work by the conviction He brings that we are God's children who have nothing to fear, and by the love, peace and joy He gives. The Spirit's message is the same one Jesus heard at His baptism: "This is my child whom I love and with whom I am well-pleased." Any beliefs or attitudes we discover in confession that accuse, punish or demean us or any

THE FRUIT OF THE SPIRIT

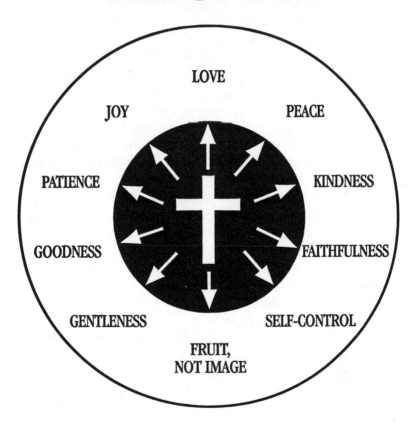

LOVE
JOY
PEACE
PATIENCE
KINDNESS
GOODNESS
FAITHFULNESS
GENTLENESS
SELF-CONTROL
FRUIT, NOT IMAGE

Galatians 5:22-23

Figure 16

other creation of God are not of the Holy Spirit! They must be resisted and challenged.

INTEGRITY REQUIRES BOUNDARIES

The second way we establish and maintain our integrity is by erecting boundaries. All of life requires boundaries. If someone offers you a drink of poison, you must say no to protect yourself. Such a boundary identifies where you begin and the rest of the world ends. We must also defend ourselves against too much of a good thing. Ice cream is not a poison, but after the first or second dish, it becomes important to say no. People encouraging us to overeat could logically say, "It's all right; it's good for you," and they would be partly right. Food is good for us. But we still have to refuse when we know more of a good thing will harm us. In a similar way, we must develop spiritual boundaries.

The world is hostile to the Spirit within us. Just as Nehemiah rebuilt the walls of Jerusalem so the Israelites could worship in safety we need "walls" to protect us. We cannot develop our identities without boundaries to keep us safe, and we can't maintain our integrity without maintaining those boundaries. Matt's indecision occurred because he didn't stop his mother and Vicki from telling him who he was and what he should do. He couldn't say no to them.

To maintain his integrity, Job had to refute the arguments and accusations of his friends. He had to refuse to "curse God and die," as his wife told him to do. His integrity had to be more important to Him than anything in life, because to have integrity is to be true to God. This cannot be compromised without losing our souls.

We saw earlier that the Spirit who descended on Jesus at His baptism is the same Spirit who inhabits and empowers us. What did Jesus do immediately after the Spirit had come upon

Him? "Jesus, full of the Holy Spirit, returned from the Jordan and was led by the Spirit in the desert, where for forty days he was tempted by the devil" (Luke 4:1-2).

He was immediately faced with having to be true to the Spirit in the face of Satan's temptations. What did He have to do to withstand them? He had to say no to rescuing Himself from the pain of being human. He had to say no to setting up a human kingdom and taking control of others. And He had to say no to avoiding responsibility and expecting God to rescue Him from human weakness. *He did not minister to others during this time.* His energy and will were used to defend His integrity against violations by Satan.

> *The only one who knows who we are is the Spirit God has placed inside us. Absolutely no one else should be trusted to establish our identity.*

We cannot experience our integrity without first exercising the power God has given us to say no to those who believe they know who we should be. The only one who knows who we are is the Spirit God has placed inside us. Absolutely no one else should be trusted to establish our identity.

God has also given us our ability to be angry as a means of defending our integrity. One of the few times Jesus was described as angry illustrates this:

> When it was almost time for the Jewish Passover, Jesus went up to Jerusalem. In the temple courts he found men selling cattle, sheep and doves, and others sitting at tables exchanging money. So he made a whip out of cords, and drove all from the temple area, both sheep and cattle; he scattered the coins of the money changers and overturned their tables. To those who sold doves he said, "Get these

out of here! How dare you turn my Father's house into a market!" (John 2:13-16).

Jesus' anger defended the integrity of God's house. Its holiness was being degraded by behavior contradictory to its identity. If such violations were allowed, its sacredness would be cheapened and its holiness defiled.

Today our bodies are the temple of the Holy Spirit (see 1 Cor. 6:19), and our integrity as God's children must be defended against those who would violate it. We, too, are sacred and must be protected from degradation. Some who try to violate us may appear well-meaning, but if they attempt to take God's place by telling us who we should or shouldn't be, they must be stopped.

Dysfunctional families are characterized by the lack of clear boundaries between people. Matt will never be able to decide what he wants to do until he can be different from his mother. As long as her expectations govern him, he can't be different, and his identity is fused with hers. As he openly rejects her attempts to control him, he will slowly discover his hopes and dreams. He will hear the quiet voice of the Spirit within as he silences the human voices drowning it out. Until that time, he can't enjoy being the person God created him to be.

An Objection?

If erecting and maintaining our boundaries is so important, why did Paul tell us to "submit to one another"? Why did Jesus tell us not to resist evil?

You have heard that it was said, "Eye for eye, and tooth for tooth." But I tell you, Do not resist an evil person. If someone strikes you on the right cheek, turn to him the other also. And if someone wants to sue you and take your tunic, let him have your cloak as well. If someone forces you to go one mile, go with him two miles (Matt. 5:38-41).

Clearly, we are not to respond to evil behavior with evil of our own. If someone attacks us violently, we are not to reply with violence. Maintaining our boundaries does not entitle us to violate others. But do these verses imply we should allow others to attack our integrity without defending it?

I have known many Christian wives and husbands who have attempted this. They gave their spouses whatever they wanted without resisting. They allowed themselves to be abused and controlled in the name of Christian submission. I don't believe that's what Christ was calling them to do. There's a difference between submitting to evil as Jesus did and submitting to someone because you believe you're worthless. Most so-called Christian submission is not done in love but in hope of having our emptiness filled by the one to whom we submit. When we allow people to violate and use us, trying to get their love, we're wearing the manipulative face of the Rescuer. We're allowing them to behave irresponsibly so they will continue to like us.

Rescuing is conforming to the world, not obeying the Spirit. We can recognize this by the fruit it bears. Submitting to the cruelty or irresponsibility of a spouse does not produce the fruit of the Spirit in a family. It produces fear, shame, malice and death. To say that Christ calls us to submit blindly to others is to abdicate our responsibility. We are not called to obey the letter of the law, even in the words of Jesus. We are called to obey the same Spirit He obeyed.

Turning the other cheek is foolhardy when done separately from the Spirit. It is nonsense to allow others to abuse us in human terms, for it serves no purpose. It's demeaning and damages our integrity.

Yet paradoxically, as we know and obey the Spirit, turning the other cheek can have eternal meaning and bear tremendous fruit. In obedience to the Spirit, we can maintain our integrity even as our bodies are destroyed. Our submission is to flow from the strength given us by the Spirit. Jesus' submission on the cross was an act of strength, not weakness. We're not to submit so as to achieve some goal, but in response to the Spirit's personal call to us. Jesus did not submit to evil until His time had come, resisting it in the desert but surrendering to it on the cross.

We likewise are to resist evil to establish and maintain our integrity as God's children until we know and hear His Spirit clearly. The service the Spirit then calls us to will be uniquely ours. It will include service to others and turning the other cheek, but only the Spirit can tell us when and how.

SAYING NO TO ALL HUMAN CLAIMS

Our boundaries must protect us from being conformed "any longer to the pattern of this world" (Rom. 12:2). Most of us do a good job of saying no to obviously sinful practices, at least those that would be observed publicly. We won't have too much difficulty refusing to rob a bank or kill our neighbors. But this falls far short of establishing the boundaries necessary to maintaining our integrity as sons of God.

We must also erect boundaries to keep good things from becoming gods. Like Paul, we must relinquish all claims to righteousness and trust completely in Christ:

If anyone else thinks he has reasons to put confidence in the flesh, I have more: circumcised on the eighth day, of the people of Israel, of the tribe of Benjamin, a Hebrew of Hebrews; in regard to the law, a Pharisee; as for zeal, persecuting the church; as for legalistic righteousness, faultless. But whatever was to my profit I now consider loss for the sake of Christ. What is more, I consider everything a loss compared to the surpassing greatness of knowing Christ Jesus my Lord, for whose sake I have lost all things. I consider them rubbish, that I may gain Christ and be found in him, not having a righteousness of my own that comes from the law, but that which is through faith in Christ—the righteousness that comes from God and is by faith (Phil. 3:4-9).

In this confession of faith, Paul relinquished all claims to righteousness based on biblical, cultural or family standards. We are called to do the same. If our sense of righteousness comes from being Protestant, Catholic, American, law-abiding or loyal to family, we are refusing to abandon ourselves to God. We must say a clear no to those lest they seduce us into idolizing them. Everything must be subordinate to Christ.

Loyalty to our country can be a good thing, but when its actions contradict our understanding of God's call, we must say no. Loving spouse and children is a very good thing, but when our loyalty requires us to behave in ways contradictory to His Spirit, we must say no.

The things that become our false gods aren't bad in and of themselves. Even the exercise of power has its appropriate place. When we look to our idols to deal with our inner emptiness, however, we compromise our integrity and sacrifice our true selves. All of them offer temporary comfort and security, but none satisfy.

BREAKING FREE FROM FAMILY

The most difficult boundary to erect is the one that acknowledges that our families are not God. This is painful, because family provided our only security during our developing years. We seldom consider Christ's directive to "hate" father and mother, wife and children, and brothers and sisters (see Luke 14:26).

His call seems too harsh, for hating them would hurt them. Yet He said that those who have left their families will be rewarded in the kingdom of God: "'I tell you the truth,' Jesus said to them, 'no one who has left home or wife or brothers or parents or children for the sake of the kingdom of God will fail to receive many times as much in this age and, in the age to come, eternal life'" (Luke 18:29-30).

Jesus was stating a deep psychological truth. *We cannot serve the kingdom of God without emotionally and spiritually breaking free of our families.* They can no longer be our gods. Dysfunctional family patterns reveal our desperate need to abandon the expectations they imposed on us. In telling us to hate them Jesus called us to hate those beliefs and expectations that keep us from being God's children.[3] We must leave them emotionally and give up our attempts to demonstrate our righteousness in the ways we've been taught. We must shift our allegiance to Jesus Christ, for only in Him can we be who God created us to be.

Breaking free of our parents can also be troubling because it seems contradictory to Christ's directive to "honor your father and mother" (Luke 18:20). To honor our parents means to treat them with respect and honesty. It does *not* mean to pretend we love them while we hide feelings of hurt, anger or bitterness. If we truly honor them, we will reveal our honest feelings in the hope of developing a real relationship. This can be incredibly frightening and difficult if we fear our parents' rejection or believe we're responsible for their feelings. But distorting the commandment to mean you shouldn't think, feel or express anything that might cause your parents pain is to give them the status of gods. If the early Hebrew Christians had tried to live without bringing pain to their parents, they would not have become Christians.

An exercise I frequently use in counseling sessions illustrates the difficulty in breaking free. Let's assume I'm working with Matt. I begin by saying, "Matt, I'd like you to picture your mother sitting in the room with us. Imagine she's sitting in the sofa or the chair here. Now, with her here, go through the list of emotions at the end of chapter 5, and identify which you feel with her present."

After a pause, Matt responds, "Well, if she's listening to our conversation, I imagine she's surprised, upset and uncomfortable." Can you see what Matt has done? I asked him what *his* emotions would be, and he has responded by telling me *his mother's emotions.* This is not unusual among

> *There is no way you can hear the Spirit within if you're busy taking care of the feelings of others.*

people who are strongly codependent. They know the emotions of others better than they know their own.

Why does this happen? At a very early age, they learned to care for their parents' needs rather than their own. They were dependent on them and learned to do this to please them. Can you see why it would be difficult for Matt to say no to his mother? He can't establish his boundaries until he first gets to know himself. Shifting our allegiance from our parents to the Spirit is part of what Jesus meant when He said we must hate our families.

As always, there's a paradox in Jesus' call to hate family. Those of us who have worn a facade in relating to our parents, if we're honest, will realize we've had little true feeling for them as persons. We don't really love them if we've been trying to be the "good child." But once we put up boundaries to protect ourselves from their expectations and trust the Spirit within us, we develop the ability to love. We need no longer play a role, and, in our freedom, we can see them as real people with frailties and pain like our own. We can now see them as God's children, because we no longer believe they're gods.

As you develop your personal boundaries and begin to trust the Spirit, I pray that your honesty and growth will draw you closer to your family. Sadly, and all too often, parents and siblings intensely resist honesty. They will refuse to believe the feelings you're discovering within and even deny you feel them. This is extremely painful and takes much time to work through. Following Christ as His child often brings division to families. Jesus predicted this clearly:

> Do you think I came to bring peace on earth? No, I tell you, but division. From now on there will be five in one family divided against each other, three against two and two against three. They will be divided, father against son and son against father, mother against daughter and daughter against mother, mother-in-law against daughter-in-law and daughter-in-law against mother-in-law (Luke 12:51-53).

If you, because of your relationship with God, begin to behave differently from what your family expects, you may end up alone. This even happens in families that identify themselves as Christian. If you decide there are issues you must talk to your family about so you can become free of some negative impact on you, find people to support you through the experience.

DECIDING WHEN TO SAY NO

If you haven't been allowed to develop protective boundaries, it can be difficult to know where to begin. I'm often asked, "When should I say no?" My answer is simple: Say no whenever you don't want to do something or believe it will be harmful to you. Be true to yourself. This sounds easy but is very difficult to do.

It takes time and effort to recognize your feelings if you've been disconnected from them. But *there is no way you can bear the Spirit within if you're busy taking care of the feelings of others.* For Matt to get in touch with the Spirit, he must first tell his mother, "No, Mom, I won't be taking care of your feelings anymore. You'll have to develop strength enough to hear who I really am. You'll have to develop your own relationship with God!" Mom won't like this. She has used Matt to protect her from reality and rescue her from pain. She's either going to have to grow up or find a new Rescuer.

Matt will feel incredibly guilty when he first says no, especially to his mother. This guilt is based on the lie that he can be God for her. He is so trapped in the Rescuer role that he's alienated from his true self and the light within.

Matt must begin with the process of confession described in chapter 5, remind himself of his new identity in Jesus Christ, and begin to say no when he wants. In refusing to play the Rescuer, he is refusing to play god and resisting Satan in the same way Jesus did in the wilderness.

BECOMING ROOTED AND ESTABLISHED

The third step in developing integrity is trusting and nurturing the Spirit of God within. Once you have established boundaries defining where you begin and the world ends, you can enjoy being God's child. In the safety provided by your "walls," you can grow in the strength and knowledge of who you are in Christ.

This is like building a barrier around a young tree to protect it from wind. When it's young and slender and its roots are shallow, strong winds can knock it down. But with a barrier protecting it, it has time to send its roots deep into the soil, becoming established and stable. We must grow in a similar way.

So then, just as you received Christ Jesus as Lord, continue to live in him, rooted and built up in him, strengthened in the faith as you were taught, and overflowing with thankfulness. See to it that no one takes you captive through hollow and deceptive philosophy, which depends on human tradition and the basic principles of this world rather than on Christ. For in Christ all the fullness of the Deity lives in bodily form, and you have been given fullness in Christ, who is the head over every power and authority (Col. 2:6-10).

As we begin to relax and enjoy being God's children, our times of silence must always include confession and the continuing death of our old selves. But as our new selves emerge, we can rejoice in the fullness of God. We can commune in peace with the One who loves us, because we understand and recognize the Spirit's voice more readily. We're less likely to confuse the messages of guilt, shame and fear with the voice of the Spirit, for we have come to know His love.

Enjoying our love relationship with God is to be the foundation of our lives. We are secure in His kingdom within. Communing with His Spirit, we discover new things about ourselves and about God that enrich and renew us. We are learning the simplicity of trusting God.

Do not worry about your life, what you will eat; or about your body, what you will wear. Life is more than food, and the body more than clothes. Consider the ravens: They do not sow or reap, they have no storeroom or barn; yet God feeds them. And how much more valuable are you than birds! Who of you by worrying can add a single hour to his life? Since you cannot do this very little thing, why do you worry about the rest? (Luke 12:22-26).

When Jesus called us to be like the "lilies of the field," He was calling us to simplicity of being. Our being in Christ must *precede* our doing. The more we trust the reality of who we are, the more the strength of His Spirit becomes available within us. The roots of His love for us and ours for Him grow deep and secure.

Eventually His voice calls us to move out from the silence and security and share the love we've discovered with others. His integrity and strength have prepared us to be His people in the world, assertive but vulnerable. Then our inward journey bears fruit in the outward journey of servant ministry.

FOR PERSONAL REFLECTION

Developing integrity includes saying no to others. Consider your Christian walk, and ask yourself, "Whom or what have I said no to in order to maintain my integrity as God's child?"

Then ask yourself to whom or what you must say no to now to develop or maintain your integrity. Have you clearly defined who you are, or are you in a state of confusion about this?

Take any unanswered or disturbing responses to these questions into confession and prayer.

FOR GROUP DISCUSSION

Answer the following questions individually, then discuss your responses.
1. In what situations do you find it most difficult to maintain your boundaries (i.e. to say no)?
2. What makes it difficult for you to say no? Is it fear of rejection or disapproval, or do you feel guilty for bringing discomfort or pain to others?
3. Try to identify one situation where you believe it's especially important for you to say no right now. Open this up for discussion, guidance and prayer.
4. If you can identify a time when you began to establish

boundaries for yourself and, as a result, began to more clearly hear and respond to the Spirit, please describe it. This can be very encouraging to others.

7
MATURITY
FREE AND RESPONSIBLE

He...gave some to be apostles, some
to be prophets, some to be evangelists,
and some to be pastors and teachers,
to prepare God's people for works of
service, so that the body of Christ may
be built up until we all reach unity
in the faith and in the knowledge of
the Son of God and become mature,
attaining to the whole measure of
the fullness of Christ.
—Ephesians 4:11-13

IN the last chapter, I compared developing integrity to the growth of a young tree. The immature tree's roots are shallow, its trunk thin and fragile. It needs protection to survive. In a similar way, when we're immature, we need boundaries to protect us from others' expectations and demands so we can develop integrity.

As a tree's roots go deep into the soil, however, and its trunk becomes large and strong, it can stand on its own. Likewise, mature people have a well-developed sense of identity, so the "winds" of disapproval, hardship or expectations will no longer "knock them down."

A tree also demonstrates maturity by bearing fruit. It draws life from the earth and creates fruit, expressing its identity. An apple tree bears apples and an orange tree, oranges. Because a tree clings to its source of life, it reproduces itself and the life it has been given through its fruit.

Bearing fruit is also the mark of maturity in people. As our integrity is protected and the Spirit within is trusted, life-giving power emerges and flows into the bearing of fruit and bringing life to others.

DYSFUNCTIONAL FAMILY PATTERNS VERSUS MATURITY

As we've seen, all families are dysfunctional to some extent. Parenting tends to focus on the "doing" of children rather than their "being." The expectations and needs of parents and society determine which actions are acceptable, and the true nature of children is repressed in shame.

We expect God to relate to us in the same manner. We

unconsciously believe He is interested only in what we *do* rather than loving us for who we *are*. It's difficult to accept that in God's kingdom, our worth, belonging and competence are given as gifts; we don't earn them by doing the right things. Instead, we're encouraged to be like the passive "lilies of the field" and leave our hurried lives of doing to enter the calm sanity of God's love.

The world's focus on doing can lead us to develop a counterfeit maturity. It isn't at all like the mature fruit-bearing tree but more like the typical Christmas tree.

> *O*ur doing is to result from the being Christ places within us through His Holy Spirit.

I like a Christmas tree but it represents the world's image of life better than it does God's. The Christmas tree has been cut off from its roots and the soil that bring it life. It has been propped up artificially rather than standing in its God-given strength. Once it has been cut off from life and artificially supported, it is then decorated with ornaments and lights to make it look attractive. The decorations are totally unrelated to the life and identity of the tree, but the world likes their appearance.

When we decorate our family Christmas tree in December, our orange tree, with its dark green leaves and bright orange decorations, goes virtually unnoticed. The miracle of its life, maturity and productivity is taken for granted and ignored. While the orange tree is most beautiful and productive, the Christmas tree is dying in our living room—and it's the center of attention. Its needles are drying up, and its decorations couldn't provide the nourishment of a single orange, but it's beautiful. For a brief time, the Christmas tree is almost an object of worship. Then, when its usefulness ends, we toss it out with our garbage.

The Christmas tree is like the counterfeit maturity produced by dysfunctional humanity. We are more interested in appearances than reality. We value education, wealth and success rather than the development of genuine, life-giving fruit from within. What the world calls maturity is a facade.

To see real maturity, we must look to Jesus Christ. Our doing is to result from the being Christ places within us through His Holy Spirit. Then the fruit we bear will not only be unique to who we are, but also true to the identity of Jesus Christ. It will be the doing of a servant.

JESUS REVEALS MATURITY

It was the Last Supper. Jesus was about to be crucified. He was sharing His last meal with His disciples, and He wanted them to remember Him and His teachings. He told them much about who they were and how to live, but His most-telling lesson had few words: "Jesus knew that the Father had put all things under his power, and that he had come from God and was returning to God" (John 13:3).

Jesus knew He was God's Son. He came from God, was going back to God, and had been entrusted with everything by God. From that secure knowledge flowed His actions, emerging from His identity just as fruit emerges from a tree. "So he got up from the meal, took off his outer clothing, and wrapped a towel around his waist. After that, he poured water into a basin and began to wash his disciples' feet, drying them with the towel that was wrapped around him" (John 13:4-5).

Simon Peter protested at this. Jesus' behavior made no sense, because he'd never seen it before—a person in authority washing the feet of those under him. Christ was breaking the rules, modeling behavior that doesn't come naturally in this world. And Peter's honest reaction was to refuse to participate because it seemed so wrong. Jesus explained His servant action later:

When he had finished washing their feet, he put on his clothes and returned to his place. "Do you understand what I have done for you?" he asked them. "You call me 'Teacher' and 'Lord,' and rightly so, for that is what I am. Now that I, your Lord and Teacher, have washed your feet, you also should wash one another's feet. I have set you an example that you should do as I have done for you. I tell you the truth, no servant is greater than his master, nor is a messenger greater than the one who sent him. Now that you know these things, you will be blessed if you do them" (John 13:12-17).

In serving, Jesus modeled the behavior of the Son of God. He told us that if He, the Master, served, we should not decide we're greater than He and need not serve. Like Him, as sons of God, we are also to serve. Our being results in our actions, not the reverse. We do not serve to become sons; we *are* sons, so we serve.

Later that evening, Jesus identified the behavior He modeled as a new commandment: "A new command I give you: Love one another. As I have loved you, so you must love one another. All men will know that you are my disciples if you love one another" (John 13:34,35).

Notice that this is not the Golden Rule: "Do unto others as you would have them do unto you." It isn't "Love your neighbor as yourself." This is a new commandment, for it orders us to love one another *as Christ loved us.* We are now to follow Christ's example of love rather than our own.

The love of Christ goes beyond accepting one another as sons of God, as crucial as that is. It extends itself to sacrificing for others. Jesus humbled Himself and took the form of a servant in washing the feet of His friends. He accepted death on the cross for our salvation. And we are commanded to love as He loved. It isn't optional for God's children.

Here is the test by which we can make sure that we know him: do we keep his commands? The man who says, "I know him", while he disobeys his commands, is a liar and a stranger to the truth; but in the man who is obedient to his word, the divine love has indeed come to its perfection....

A man may say "I am in the light," but if he hates his brother, he is still in the dark. Only the man who loves his brother dwells in the light: there is nothing in him to make him stumble (1 John 2:3-5, 9-10; *NEB*).

To become mature will be to love others as Christ loves us, just as He commanded. Obedience is our path to maturity.

BARRIERS TO OBEDIENCE

For most of us, being told to obey does not elicit positive feelings. Words like "command" and, especially, "obey" trigger responses that hamper obedience, because we envision a God like our parents. No matter how good they may have been, they didn't parent as God does, for human parents often wear the three faces of sin.

If we were neglected by our parents, we're likely to expect that God doesn't love us. Our intellectual belief may be that He cares, but we won't *feel* it. If a parent was a Rescuer and protected us from the consequences of our actions, we'll expect God to protect us from pain, and we'll become angry when He doesn't. If a parent played the Victim, we may be hesitant to act in ways that we fear will hurt God.

These are a few examples of how our relationship with our parents can lead us to misunderstand God and so remain immature. This is one of the reasons God chose to enter our world in the person of Jesus. Only in Him do we see an accurate human model of the parenting of God the Father. The more we know of Him and His love, the more we'll realize how totally different from any human parent He is. Jesus told many stories and parables to reveal the Father, but none corrects our misperceptions more accurately than the story of the prodigal son.

FREE AND RESPONSIBLE

To mature, we must first be free to be immature. God allows us this freedom, just as the father of the prodigal son did for his child.

There was a man who had two sons. The younger one said to his father, "Father, give me my share of the estate." So he divided his property between them.

Not long after that, the younger son got together all he had, set off for a distant country and there squandered his wealth in wild living. After he had spent everything, there was a severe famine in that whole country, and he began to be in need. So he went and hired himself out to a citizen of that country, who sent him to his fields to feed pigs. He longed to fill his stomach with the pods that the pigs were eating, but no one gave him anything.

When he came to his senses, he said, "How many of my father's hired men have food to spare, and here I am starving to death! I will set out and go back to my father and say to him: Father, I have sinned against heaven and against you. I am no longer worthy to be called your son; make me like one of your hired men." So he got up and went to his father.

But while he was still a long way off, his father saw him and was filled with compassion for him; he ran to his son, threw his arms around him and kissed him.

The son said to him, "Father, I have sinned against heaven and against you. I am no longer worthy to be called your son."

But the father said to his servants, "Quick! Bring the best robe and put it on him. Put a ring on his finger and sandals on his feet. Bring the fattened calf and kill it. Let's have a feast and celebrate. For this son of mine was dead and is alive again; he was lost and is found." So they began to celebrate (Luke 15:11-24).

Human fathers don't give their children that much freedom. The prodigal's father gave him all the blessings and power of a son yet allowed him to waste them sinfully. He gave him the freedom to mess up his life completely. He did not view his son's behavior as a reflection on him but let him make mistakes. Then, after the young man's inheritance was thoroughly wasted, the father didn't point out his foolishness or say, "I told you so." There was no condemnation!

How did the son use his freedom? He did things his own way, sleeping with prostitutes and squandering all he'd been given. When the pleasure was over, he faced the consequences of his own decisions. He had no one to blame. *The freedom given by his father revealed his immaturity.* He could learn the lesson he needed, because it wasn't muddled with "shoulds." He wanted to do it, he did it, and he experienced the results.

Because of his freedom, he realized the love and security he had with his father and returned repentant and vulnerable. He was ready to receive the love that had been there all along and that welcomed and rejoiced in his return.

In Jesus Christ, we have been granted this same freedom! We can sin, and God's love in Christ is available for us. We're free to do whatever we want; we make the decisions and live with the consequences.

An Objection?

You may want to protest by saying, "You're implying that sin is a good thing—that we should rebel." No! Rebellion against God is horrible. It brings pain, alienation and death. Good can be resurrected from sin only because of what God has done in Jesus. He has used our transgressions as opportunity to reveal the depth of His love.

We must never forget the price Christ paid for our freedom. If we take His commands lightly, we're blind to the suffering sin produces. It was not good that the prodigal wasted his inheritance and damaged his life and the lives of others. It was tragic. But the father's graceful response revealed his love in a way the son could not have known without sinning.

It can be frightening to realize we are free to live as we choose and are responsible for the results. If no one tells us what to do and how to do it, we have no one else to blame when things go wrong. We're so used to blaming that it's hard to remember all blame has been carried by Christ on the cross. We need fear mistakes or failure no longer, because Christ has taken all sin onto Himself, and it is dead. It no longer has any power over you or me. Yet we continually try to resurrect sin by being afraid of God and afraid to act.

We fear freedom because we believe, somewhere deep inside, that sin is actually better than obedience. We fear that if we're free, we'll eat the forbidden fruit of sexual immorality, for example, and like it better than we do living for Christ. The simple truth, however, is that if we pursue it, *we will eventually realize our folly.* That's why God dared to set us free. He knows He's offering everything we need and is willing to trust us to discover it.

We can be confident that everything works together for good. Our actions will either be consistent with God's goodness or, if sinful, will lead to consequences revealing our need for God's forgiveness and love. When we discover our sin and entrust it to Christ, God's love penetrates our souls to new depths, and another part of us is added to God's kingdom. We then want to obey in that area because we *know* God and His commands can be trusted.

Thus, it isn't our sin that develops our maturity, but God's loving response to it. Sin is not a good thing, but freedom is. We live in a world filled with the beauty of God's creation and marred by the ugliness of sin. The good news is that life and beauty have won.

As Robert Farrar Capon writes:

> If we are ever to enter fully into the glorious liberty of the sons of God, we are going to have to spend more time thinking about freedom than we do. The church, by and large, has had a poor record of encouraging freedom. She has spent so much time inculcating in us the fear of making mistakes that she has made us like ill-taught piano students: we play our songs, but we never really hear them because our main concern is not to make music but to avoid some flub that will get us in dutch. She has been so afraid we will lose sight of the laws of our nature that she has made us care more about how we look than about who we are—made us act more like the subjects of a police state than fellow citizens of the saints.[1]

We have been set free in Jesus Christ. "So if the Son sets you free, you will be free indeed" (John 8:36).

A few years ago, I had opportunity to discuss my faith with a Jewish acquaintance. She asked me why I was a Christian and what it meant to be one. I explained that Christ had experienced the consequences of sin for me and that I was forever forgiven. When I said I no longer had to feel anxious about God's love for me and could trust myself to Him, she protested. That was too easy, she insisted; we have to earn our way into God's favor by the things we do. The freedom I described was unacceptable to her.

This "fight not to be free" is exactly what Paul encountered as he struggled to convince the early Christians to accept their freedom in Christ.

> Before you Gentiles knew God you were slaves to so-called gods that did not even exist. And now that you have found God (or I should say that God has found you), how can it be that you want to go back again and become slaves once more to another poor, weak, useless religion of trying to get to heaven by obeying God's laws? (Gal. 4:8,9, *TLB*).

We do not have to *do* a thing to be loved by God. We are in Jesus Christ, and in Him we are loved and free. Christ died for us while we were yet sinners! Capon says we unconsciously amend Scripture to fit our expectations something like this: "But God commendeth his love toward us, in that, while we were yet sinners, Christ died for us, on the condition that after a reasonable length of time we would be the kind of people no one would ever have to die for in the first place. Otherwise the whole deal is off."[2]

We misread the Bible in this way because we're used to conditional love. We expect that people love us only to get what they want. *God doesn't love conditionally*. He didn't have us sign a contract that said, "I will die for you on the condition that if I do it, you will stop your sinning." This is ridiculous, because He knew we couldn't stop if we tried!

He died, not *expecting* us to stop sinning, but to give us a way of *dealing with the sin* in our lives. We no longer have to fret about our sins, because we now have someone "who speaks to the Father in our defense—Jesus Christ, the Righteous One" (1 John 2:1). We have been set free from the power of sin, so we need no longer fear judgment but can feel secure as God's children and grow to maturity.

Paradoxically, freedom to sin enables us to stop sinning. The grace and love demonstrated in granting our forgiveness reveals our security in God's love, so we no longer need to try to gain life through our own means. Attempting to do it on our own creates all sinful behavior. If we truly realize the freedom God's love grants, sin loses its allure. It gradually is exposed for what it is—death! "For if you live according to the sinful nature, you will die; but if by the Spirit you put to death the misdeeds of the body, you will live" (Rom. 8:13).

Jesus told the woman caught in adultery that He would not condemn her, and then He said, "Do not sin again." We, too, are told not to sin, because *sin is not good for us*. It brings pain and death into our lives, and God doesn't want that for us. Paul could not have said it more clearly than he did to the Corinthians: "'I am free to do anything' you say. Yes, but not everything is for my good. No doubt I am free to do anything, but I for one will not let anything make free with me" (1 Cor. 6:12, *NEB*).

Paul called us to recognize our freedom and the responsibility that goes with it. We are free to sin and free to experience the consequences of sinning. We are free to be prodigal sons.

CREATIVE TENSION: BEING SHAPED BY GOD

What a strange situation we are in! We have been commanded to love and yet left free to disobey. Pastor Earl Palmer says, "We live in a tension between being a whole human being including our emotions and sins and God's claim on us including His moral law."[3] That tension forces us to "work out our salvation with fear and trembling" (see Phil. 2:12). When we acknowledge and live in this tension, we mature. When we avoid it, we remain undeveloped.

God uses this tension as a potter uses his hands to shape clay. The potter's hands exert pressure to form the clay into the shape he envisions. The clay resists and responds to the pressure because of its unique characteristics. Its texture, density and pliability all participate in the creative process. *If the clay does not resist and respond to the potter's hands, he cannot create.* If it does not "push back," it lacks substance and integrity and will remain without form.

> *The most important issue in developing maturity is to understand that honesty with God is more important than appearances. He would rather we be openly defiant than pretend we love Him.*

Tension between the potter and his clay is essential.

In the same way, we must honestly be who we are in our relationship with God so we may become mature. We are not passive like the clay, for we've been given the power not only to resist, but even to rebel. We're to use that power to be actively involved with Him. As long as we stay open and honest, He can use even our rebellion for His purposes.

OPEN REBELLION BETTER THAN PIOUS PRETENSE

Too often we avoid the tension by trying to fool ourselves and God into believing we're obeying. We do all the right things, but not out of love. We appear to be obedient until events reveal our true spirit. The prodigal's older brother seemed obedient until his father's love exposed his real attitude. I can identify easily with his response:

Meanwhile, the older son was in the field. When he came

near the house, he heard music and dancing. So he called one of the servants and asked him what was going on. "Your brother has come," he replied, "and your father has killed the fattened calf because he has him back safe and sound."

The older brother became angry and refused to go in. So his father went out and pleaded with him. But he answered his father, "Look! All these years I've been slaving for you and never disobeyed your orders. Yet you never gave me even a young goat so I could celebrate with my friends. But when this son of yours who has squandered your property with prostitutes comes home, you kill the fattened calf for him!"

"My son," the father said, "you are always with me, and everything I have is yours. But we had to celebrate and be glad, because this brother of yours was dead and is alive again; he was lost and is found" (Luke 15:25-32).

I know exactly how he felt. He had been a good boy all his life and looked around to see the bad getting all the goodies. Those of us who have played the Rescuer role often feel this way. The bargain we thought we struck with our parents and with life was that if we were good, we would be rewarded. It isn't necessarily so.

We believe we've earned our way to righteousness and expect God to follow through. We have hidden our deep need for God and set out to be good on our own merits. This is the essence of sin. We've hidden it so well, however, that our true spirit can't be seen until we don't get what we believe we've earned. Then we're angry, and our anger reveals our motives. We are being good to get what we want, not because of our love for God. We appear to be giving up everything but are actually holding back our true selves. That way we can look good without paying the price. The early church witnessed a clear example of such hypocrisy:

> Now a man named Ananias, together with his wife Sapphira, also sold a piece of property. With his wife's full knowledge he kept back part of the money for himself, but brought the rest and put it at the apostles' feet.
>
> Then Peter said, "Ananias, how is it that Satan has so filled your heart that you have lied to the Holy Spirit and have kept for yourself some of the money you received for the land? Didn't it belong to you before it was sold? And after it was sold, wasn't the money at your disposal? What made you think of doing such a thing? You have not lied to men but to God."
>
> When Ananias heard this, he fell down and died. And great fear seized all who heard what had happened (Acts 5:1-5).

Pretending with God is not wise. We can die from it. Peter pointed out to Ananias that he never had to give all the money to God. He was free to give only a portion of it or not to give at all. It was his money. But rather than honestly saying to God, "I want to give you this much, but I want to keep the rest for myself," Ananias pretended to give it all. He didn't realize his freedom, and it cost him.

The most important issue in developing maturity is to understand that honesty with God is more important than appearances. He would rather we be openly defiant than pretend we love Him. Paul, for example, persecuted Christians and approved of the stoning of Stephen. He never pretended to be a believer but openly attacked the Church. Yet God chose to work through Paul rather than through others who were obedient. God's choice illustrates the words of God to the church in Laodicea:

I know your deeds, that you are neither cold nor hot. I wish you were either one or the other! So, because you are lukewarm—neither hot nor cold—I am about to spit you out of my mouth. You say, "I am rich; I have acquired wealth and do not need a thing." But you do not realize that you are wretched, pitiful, poor, blind and naked. I counsel you to buy from me...salve to put on your eyes, so you can see (Rev. 3:15-18).

The prodigal's older brother likewise appeared to "have it all together," but his resentment and jealousy revealed his pretense. He was truly lukewarm in his relationship with his father rather than honestly rebellious or loving. The prodigal's relationship was stormy but real. When we're real, God can work with us; when we pretend, we maintain our blindness and lose our chance for love.

Paul Tournier, in *Adventure of Living,* says,

The greatest obstacle in the way of acceptance is the appearance of acceptance. The greatest obstacle to virtue is the appearance of virtue. The greatest obstacle to humility is the appearance of humility. The greatest obstacle to faith is the appearance of faith. The greatest obstacle to love is the appearance of love.[4]

God does not want us to avoid the tension between His commands and our sinfulness. He uses this tension to produce maturity in us. Our growth springs from our deepening realization of our emptiness and sinfulness on the one hand, and the depth of God's love on the other. We cannot know one without the other.

God intends that we use our freedom in Christ to take action. We are to obey the promptings of His Spirit when we're aware of them, knowing that, in our imperfection, our obedience will be halting and incomplete. In seeing our failings and dying to ourselves, we grow closer to Him. He won't force us to obey but desires our obedience because He loves us and knows it's best for us. As we experience who He really is, we want to obey in response.

> When I am really in conscious communion with the reality of the wild, passionate, relentless, stubborn, pursuing, tender love of God in Jesus Christ for me, then it's not that I have to or I got to or I must or I should or I ought: suddenly I want to change because I know how deeply I'm loved.[5]

THE BOLD SERVANT

Jesus has commanded us to serve one another: "If anyone wants to be first, he must be the very last, and the servant of all" (Mark 9:35). In doing so, we follow His model of what it means to be a child of God.

Do you picture a servant as passive, compliant and dependent; or as active, strong and confident? Certainly most images of human servanthood are those of the first kind. Servants are usually envisioned as powerless, weak, Mr. Milquetoast types. Nobody wants to be that kind of servant.

This negative image can make Christ's call unattractive. Unfortunately, many Christian lives lack initiative, direction and adventure because of this powerless understanding of Christian servanthood.

Such a view usually develops in childhood. Some parents are so restrictive that their children experience a steady stream of no's from when they're about one year old until they're adults. Only certain narrow behaviors are approved, and the rest are wrong. Parents may also be overly protective and restrict their children to protect them from pain. Kids from such restrictive or protective families conclude that every action is either right or wrong, good or bad, and they see the world as a fearful place.

How do you live and serve in such a world? Very carefully. You measure every action before you take it. You don't trust yourself to do the right thing, because you're never sure you know all the rules. *You seldom act on your own initiative* but instead wait for someone to tell you what to do. You live in fear and guilt because often, when you have acted on your own, you've been wrong.

I have struggled with this. *I have hesitated to act—to write this book for example, because I was afraid I might act in the wrong way or from the wrong motives.* I didn't want to make a mistake, because that would be disastrous. I was supposed to sit back and wait for God to tell me what to do and how to do it.

The years of waiting to write were very frustrating. At times, God did seem to give direction, and I felt it was safe to act. But most of the time, I felt angry, because God wasn't telling me what to do. If He didn't tell me, how could I be sure I was doing the right thing? *I was paralyzed in the name of Jesus Christ.*

Paul Tournier describes how this paralysis can become a tragic and continuing experience of failure. As we fearfully take the initiative and do something, we evaluate it negatively because of our perfectionism. We believe we must be without error to be acceptable, and now that we have taken a step of our own, sure enough, we failed. This increases our anxiety for the next attempt. "Anxiety engenders fear: fear paralyzes, breaks the spirit, takes away joy, deadens life, and engenders self-centeredness, absorbing the mind and turning it away from adventure."[6] The fear and guilt rob us of the adventure of life, and we spend our time avoiding unhappiness rather than pursuing joy, much like Charlie Brown (see fig. 17).

Figure 17

Tragically, we settle for a safe, uneventful life. This response to God is described in the parable of the talents.

[The kingdom of heaven] is like a man going abroad, who called his servants and put his capital in their hands; to one he gave five bags of gold, to another two, to another one, each according to his capacity. Then he left the country. The man who had the five bags went at once and employed them in business, and made a profit of five bags, and the man who had the two bags made two. But the man who had been given one bag of gold went off and dug a hole in the ground, and hid his master's money.

A long time afterwards their master returned, and proceeded to settle accounts with them. The man who had been given the five bags of gold came and produced the five he had made: "Master," he said, "you left five bags with me; look, I have made five more." "Well done, my good and trusty servant!" said the master. "You have proved trustworthy in a small way; I will now put you in charge of something big. Come and share your master's delight."

The man with the two bags then came and said, "Master, you left two bags with me; look, I have made two more." "Well done, my good and trusty servant!" said the master. "You have proved trustworthy in a small way; I will now put you in charge of something big. Come and share your master's delight."

Then the man who had been given one bag came and said, "Master, I knew you to be a hard man: you reap where you have not sown, you gather where you have not scattered; so I was afraid, and I went and hid your gold in the ground. Here it is—you have what belongs to you." "You lazy rascal!" said the master. "You knew that I reap where I have not sown, and gather where I have not scattered? Then you ought to have put my money on deposit,

and on my return I should have got it back with interest.
Take the bag of gold from him, and give it to the one with
the ten bags. For the man who has will always be given
more, till he has enough and to spare; and the man who
has not will forfeit even what he has. Fling the useless servant out into the dark, the place of wailing and grinding of
teeth!" (Matt. 25:14-30, *NEB*).

This parable has long disturbed me. What I thought I understood, I didn't like. I identified with the third servant, the one
who was afraid of the master and hid his talent. It didn't seem
fair that he should be punished for trying to keep himself safe
from the master's wrath. Yet the message seemed to be that we
had better use our talents in the right way or we would be punished.

As I began to understand my own emotions, however, especially my fears—and as I began to grasp the depth of God's
love and grace in Christ, the parable took on a new meaning.
Yes, the master was upset because the servant had not been
trustworthy with his talent, but why did this happen? *It happened because the third servant had a false image of the master.*
He didn't know him. He viewed the master as a hard man, reap-
ing where he did not sow and gathering where he did not scat-
ter. He saw the master as one who used people for his own
ends; as one who dominated others for his own gain. So he
feared him and was afraid to act, fearing he would do the
wrong thing and be punished.

As I realized the servant's fear and negative image of the
master had paralyzed him, I also realized why I never liked the
parable. I identified with the frightened servant because I had
the same negative view of God. I had viewed Him as a harsh,
unloving, restrictive master who would be angry if I made a
mistake. As I reread the parable viewing the master as loving
and desiring to reward his servants, I realized the master was

angry *not because the servant didn't make a profit, but because he didn't know and trust the master.*

Because of his fear, the servant lost the talent he had and ended up in darkness, in the place of wailing and gnashing of teeth. I already knew that place. I had been there a long time. My fear had kept me from using my talent, making my life dark and anxious. Unfortunately, my experience is all too common among Christians.

Is this the kind of life Christ had in mind when He said He came to bring us joy? Is fear meant to govern our lives? No. "For God hath not given us the spirit of fear; but of power, and of love, and of a sound mind" (2 Tim. 1:7, *KJV*).

As sons of God, we have nothing to fear. We have been set free from our slavery to sin and entered into a relationship with a loving Father. He has given us "talents," and we are to invest them in bold service to Him. We can even bring our fears and weaknesses to Him when they seem to overwhelm and paralyze us, for He understands.

> Since therefore we have a great high priest who has passed through the heavens, Jesus the Son of God, let us hold fast to the religion we profess. For ours is not a high priest unable to sympathize with our weaknesses, but one who, because of his likeness to us, has been tested in every way, only without sin. Let us therefore boldly approach the throne of our gracious God, where we may receive mercy and in his grace find timely help (Heb. 4:14-16, *NEB*).

How do we live once we realize we're truly free? Martin Luther said it in a way I am sure was intended to shock his readers: "Sin boldly, but believe and rejoice in Christ more boldly still." A few years ago, this would have upset me, for I would not have understood. He wasn't saying we should go out and purposely do sinful things, then trust God's grace to "get us off

Figure 18

the hook." He was emphasizing that if we choose to act at all, we can't avoid sinning.

We're human; we will make mistakes. We'll act from the wrong motives. We'll hurt people even when our motives are pure. We'll manipulate people without knowing it. If we intend to wait until we can act perfectly, *we will never act at all.* So Luther was saying we should go ahead and live our lives boldly, without fear, knowing we will sin but giving the sin and blame to Christ on the cross and rejoicing in His forgiveness. Lucy offers a practical perspective on the matter (see fig. 18).

God's Plan

You may want to protest at this point, "But isn't it true that God has a plan for my life and will guide me according to that plan?" Yes, God has a plan in that He wants us to love and serve one another, and He'll guide us as we live our daily lives. Rarely, however, does He tell us what to do when we're not already in motion. Tournier says it in this way: "God guides us when we are on the way, not when we are standing still, just as one cannot steer a car unless it is moving."[7]

Certainly there are times when we're to wait on the Lord. We must be careful not to put the cart before the horse again and spend all our time *doing* while ignoring our relationship with Him, which is the source of our integrity. If we neglect our *being,* our doing will quickly become empty and exhausting.

As we hear God's voice, however, we must act. When we're moving in obedience to what we *do* understand, He can guide us into deeper understanding, more fruitful obedience and greater adventure.

God wants us to be responsive and responsible servants. Dietrich Bonhoeffer described the world as "the sphere of concrete responsibility given to us by and in Jesus Christ."[8] We are to take initiative and make the possible happen, even knowing we will often mess it up. I have sometimes wished the parable of the talents had described a fourth servant who went out with his talent and invested it, desiring to earn additional talents for his master, but the business failed. He returned to the master without even the talent he was given in the first place. How do you believe the master would have greeted this news?

I believed at one time that the servant would have been in big trouble, that the master would have been furious and punished him for making a mistake. Now I believe he would have been deeply pleased by the servant's desire to produce for him and would have welcomed him, encouraged him, and given him another talent with which to try again.

> *Obedience is not an option; it's a necessity. But obedience without relationship with God is hypocrisy.*

As I pondered this addition to the parable, I became frustrated with God for not having written it my way so I would have understood. Why didn't He include someone who did his best but still messed up so we could see the Master's response? *I believe He didn't include it because if we step out as His servants, responding to His love, He will produce the fruit.* All we need do is cling to the vine of Christ and allow the life-giving "sap" of the Holy Spirit to motivate us, and fruit will be produced through us. "It is the man who shares my life and whose life I share who proves fruitful" (see John 15:5, *NEB*). We have nothing to fear! Our productivity as His servants is guaranteed; all we need do is act.

> God's training is for now, not presently. His purpose is for this minute, not for something in the future. We have nothing to do with the afterwards of obedience; we get wrong when we think of the afterwards. What men call training and preparation, God calls the end.

God's end is to enable me to see that He can walk on the chaos of my life just now. If we have a further end in view, we do not pay sufficient attention to the immediate present: if we realize that obedience is the end, then each moment as it comes is precious.[9]

We don't have to try to create fruit ourselves or work to be like Christ. We're not to imitate Christ but are to live in Him and He in us. We won't have to set out to "do" the fruit of the Spirit because we have to, but we'll discover fruit emerging as a part of us. The fruit will be "added unto us" as we seek the kingdom of God (see Matt. 6:33). We will *be* like Christ rather than trying to *do* like him.

OBEDIENCE: OUR KEY TO LIFE

Obedience is the key to maintaining our freedom and experiencing our new identity. It is not the obedience of a coercive slavery but of a loving, Father-son relationship. *His commands are best for us* and are given because He wants us to enjoy life and continue in our freedom.

By changing God's commands to "voluntary guidelines," liberal Christianity has attempted to alleviate the tension between God's commands and our sinfulness. But reducing God's claim on us turns Christianity into a religion of "being sincere" rather than knowing and obeying the true God.

Christian faith without obedience offers no challenge. It becomes a bland, lifeless religion with no real claim on us, for it is based simply on "doing our best." Taking His commands seriously, however, deepens our realization of emptiness and sin and reveals our need for Him and His healing. We cannot receive life without being confronted by Him.

Obedience is not an option; it's a necessity. But obedience without relationship with God is hypocrisy. We must be honest.

If we don't want to obey, let's not fake it. Let's say a frank no to God and enter into dialogue with Him. In many cases, we'll discover the god we said no to was not the true God after all. It was a false, human-developed image we must reject. We may discover our no to the one we feared was God was actually inspired by the Spirit.

If we feel resistant or rebellious, let's go to Him, confess it, and wait for His response. After a time, He may direct us to obey even though we don't want to, but then it won't be hypocrisy. It will be an honest decision based on a relationship rather than a desire to "appear" Christian. We will have faced ourselves and Him openly. He wants *us*, not just our obedience.

Christ in the Garden of Gethsemane was our perfect model for this type of relationship. In Luke 22:42 He said, "Father, if you are willing, take this cup from me; yet not my will, but yours be done." Another way of saying this would be, "Father, I don't really *want* to do what I'm being told to do. Yet I want to be faithful to You." He went on in conversation with the Father and sweat drops of blood in His anguish. The struggle was intense. But He chose to obey as a response of love to the Father.

When the Lord creates even a small desire to obey within us, we must act. If we neglect those sparks of understanding and love, we rob ourselves of freedom and joy. We either act in obedience or return to Him with our resistance and talk to Him about it, because we belong to Him, and He loves us.

What Will You Do with Your Freedom?

God has created you with unique abilities and desires. No other person has walked your path or experienced your pain. God has reached out to you, offering love, healing and life. As you respond to His grace and receive His forgiveness, He commands you to love others as He has loved you. He calls you to enter His kingdom by obeying Him and enjoying the life He gives.

Yet God also grants you the freedom to express yourself in whatever way you choose. You can even refuse Him. What will you do with your freedom?

When I act in my freedom, I often neglect the Spirit within me. I decorate myself like a Christmas tree while I cut off my roots and begin to die. I soon feel anxious and empty. In the past, I would have felt guilty and ashamed about doing this. Now I'm grateful for the freedom and recognize the anxiety and emptiness as symptoms revealing that I need my roots. I return to Him just as the prodigal son returned to his father, reaching out for his forgiveness and love.

I've done this thousands of times. Each time has brought a new lesson and a deeper experience of His love. Gradually, through the years, the things I want to do are becoming the things He wants me to do. I can't take pride in this, because my part has been to make the mistakes! He granted the freedom; He revealed the lesson; He welcomed me back. All I've done is return to Him to receive His love. Only in recent years have I realized that the more I act, the more I grow. Being paralyzed by fear robs us of life and the lessons we can learn from it.

God wants you to mature into the fullness of His Son, Jesus Christ, by developing your talents and using your gifts. There is no right way to do that. He's given you the authority to make decisions and learn from them. I encourage you to begin where you are *now* by doing what you want to do *now.* Don't let fear stop you.

As you act, remain in His light and open to His words. He will use events, people, Scripture and His Spirit to shape you. There will be pain and suffering along the way, and these also will be used to help you grow.

You will discover He's faithful even when you're not. Slowly you'll discover how solid your foundation in Christ is, and your boldness and confidence will increase. Experience will sharpen your ability to discern when you're obeying the Spirit and when you're trying to go it alone. You'll learn to trust and obey His Spirit, and His fruit will be revealed in you. Ultimately you will "stand firm in all the will of God, mature and fully assured" (Col. 4:12).

FOR PERSONAL REFLECTION

What are you going to do with your freedom? Do you have dreams, ideas or hopes that have gone unexpressed? Take some time by yourself and explore this. Think back to childhood hopes and dreams. Have you set any of these aside prematurely?

Imagine yourself taking steps to fulfill your dream, and look through the emotions list at the end of chapter 5 to discover your emotional reactions to taking initiative in this way. Be alert to feelings of fear and guilt. As you discover your feelings about doing what you want to do, consider whether you have used God as a reason *not to do what you really desire.* God has set you free; He cannot be a reason for not doing something you really want to do. Could you be doing what the third servant in the parable of the talents did, using your fear of God as an excuse for not using responsibly the talents given you?

Take your dreams and hopes to God in prayer. Ask Him if there are ways He might use your dreams to fulfill His purposes. Consider the possibility that God has created your desires and hopes and that He can use them in ways you have never imagined.

FOR GROUP DISCUSSION

Use your time together to share the dreams and hopes you've had during your life. Examine what happened to those dreams.

As you explain, ask the rest of the group to hold you account-able. Do they think your reasons for not pursuing your dreams are valid? Does anybody suspect you may be avoiding taking responsibility for your dreams? Ask the Holy Spirit to use this time of discussion to reveal to you barriers that have been invisible. Then cooperate with Him in challenging them.

As you listen to others share their dreams, work to hear them accurately. Try to understand the barriers they've encountered, yet give them honest feedback.

If you've overcome obstacles and pursued a dream, describe the experience to the group. Especially look for ways God has used your dream that you could not have anticipated. As you look back, what do you suspect has been your part in pursuing your dream, and what has been God's?

PART FOUR

ENJOYING GOD'S FAMILY

8

INTIMACY

LOVING GOD'S FAMILY

*I no longer call you servants,
because a servant does not know
his master's business. Instead, I have
called you friends, for everything
that I learned from my Father I
have made known to you.*

—John 15:15

To be intimate with others is to reveal our innermost selves to them, including our emotions, thoughts and desires. For such deep sharing of the soul and spirit to occur, people must respect and trust each other.

Jesus has been intimate with us. He has revealed who He is and what God the Father is like. He chose to do this even though it would lead to His suffering and crucifixion. He had the power of God at His disposal and could have treated us as servants but He chose instead to treat us as friends and humble Himself for us.

Now God invites us to become one with Him. In a world controlled by sin, however, to choose to be intimate is to choose to be hurt. Yet Jesus calls us to this kind of intimacy with Him and with one another.

INTIMACY AND CONTROL

Most of us have little difficulty sharing our likes and dislikes, our activities and even our opinions. Sharing our deepest hurts, fears and desires, however, is very difficult. Most of us agree with the person who said, "I am afraid to tell you who I am, because if I tell you who I am, you may not like who I am, and it's all that I have."[1] When we reveal our deepest thoughts and feelings, we're taking the ultimate risk, for we are exposing our true selves to judgment.

If I'm too frightened to be vulnerable, I can't be intimate. Yet I still desire it. Deep inside, I desperately want to be loved. So if I'm too ashamed and frightened to open up, I settle for less than intimacy. Instead of risking more hurt, I try to get attention and interaction with others through manipulation. I try to create closeness on my terms and under my control. Instead of revealing myself, I wear the manipulative masks of the Controller, Rescuer and Victim. In the process, I destroy the very intimacy I desire. An experience I had recently illustrates this.

I was attending a workshop designed to help people experience community. Our goal was, in the words of Scott Peck, to "learn to communicate honestly with each other, and develop relationships which went deeper than our masks of composure."[2] We came together hoping to break through our barriers and be intimate. I wanted this very much.

Near the end of the workshop, I experienced a few moments of joy and

> *In a world controlled by sin,...to choose to be intimate is to choose to be hurt. Yet Jesus calls us to this kind of intimacy with Him and with one another.*

closeness different from any I had known. I sensed the absence of judgment and a developing spirit of love. I was excited and hopeful. Then someone said something I didn't like. I became angry and told him he should change his behavior if he wanted us to be intimate. I was determined to prevent him from destroying the sense of community I wanted-ed. But from that moment on, the group seemed more distant and separated than before. My magic moment was gone, and the sense of community I desired did not happen.

Later that evening, as I was thinking through the day's events, I realized what I'd done. I hadn't expressed my fear that I was going to lose what I wanted. Instead, I had tried to change the other person. I had tried to make intimacy happen my way. By trying to force people to love as I believed they should, I helped destroy my dream and robbed myself of love.

This is the tragedy of being human. We're created for love

and intimacy and can't be fulfilled without it. But our insistence on doing things our way alienates us from God and each other. We are left lonely and unfulfilled. The oneness we desire only can come as we release control and accept our place in God's family.

BLINDED BY THE NEED FOR CONTROL

You can't control what happens in an intimate relationship. You're free to be you, and, most threateningly, the other person is free as well. He or she does not have to love you.

To avoid hurt and exposure, we try to orchestrate life to make it predictable and safe. We are far too busy figuring out the "right things to do" to avoid judgment or get attention that we're seldom truly "present" with each other. And if we're not really present, we can't give or receive love. A recent crisis in my family revealed how this happens in my life.

A few months ago, my father was scheduled to have an artery leading to his heart cleared of an obstruction. The procedure is called *angioplasty*. My brother and I returned home to be with my parents while this was done.

The morning we went into the hospital, a heart surgeon introduced himself to us. "You don't want to see me again today," he said, then explained why he was present. When angioplasty is performed, it's standard practice to have a surgeon standing by to perform a bypass if the clearing procedure fails. A bypass is major surgery. The surgeon told us that only about 5 percent of angioplasty patients require bypass surgery and that everything would probably go smoothly without it. I felt both threatened and reassured.

As the angioplasty was being performed, we waited and waited. We began to suspect something was wrong; it was taking too much time. Finally the waiting room phone rang with a message for my mother. Sure enough, the angioplasty wasn't working, and they'd decided to do an arterial bypass. We were among the unlucky 5 percent.

The doctor said we could have a brief moment with my dad before he was wheeled into surgery. Thoughts raced through my head: *This might be the last time I see Dad. What should I say? Should I try to talk to him or just be silent and give him a hug? What's the right thing to do?* Rather than facing my fear and uncertainty, I tried to get control of a frightening situation I wasn't prepared to handle.

Before I knew it, I was in the hallway with my dad, and then he was gone. Moments later, I realized what had happened. Although I'd been physically with him, *I had not seen my father.* I'd been so busy deciding the right thing to say or do that I had not been truly present with him. Because I was so anxious, I'd been blind. Fortunately, the bypass was successful, and I could be with him the next day.

My experience is not unlike everyday life. We're so self-absorbed that we seldom really see the people we're with. Just as my concern about doing the right thing prevented me from seeing my father, we live without truly seeing one another, pre-occupied with ourselves, missing the beauty of life and of each other.

BLINDED BY OUR EXPECTATIONS AND NEEDS

Just as we can be blinded by trying to control we can also fail to see others because we expect them to be someone they're not. When we don't face our emptiness and need honestly, we look to others to fill them. When I unconsciously expect the person I love to my fill my needs, I'm setting our relationship up for failure, because she can't. She can only be who she is. If I'm expecting her to fill my inner void, I'll be angry when she fails. My expectations blind me to seeing her accurately and genuinely knowing her. If I allow her to be herself, she will bring me some pleasure and even fill some of my needs. But she won't fill my emptiness. She can't make me happy.

Expecting another person to make life worth living is a sure sign of a dysfunctional relationship. The love songs and romance novels say we're in love if we "can't live without" someone. They're wrong. Being unable to live without someone is codependency, not love. Our self-esteem has been invested in another rather than trusted to God and His Spirit within.

Some forms our damaging expectations can take are:

1. If you love me, you'll make me happy.
2. If you love me, you'll always want to be with me.
3. If you love me, you'll never criticize me.
4. If you love me, you'll never hurt me.
5. If you love me, you'll think and feel as I do.

These can be summarized as, "If you love me, you'll be a god for me and meet all my needs." If I unconsciously assume this, I will either take the Controller role and try to force her into loving me the way she "should," or I'll play the Victim and imply that I can't live without her doing what I need.

If I've been raised to be a Rescuer, I am more likely to go into my intimate relationships believing I should fill all my partner's needs. Then I try to be indispensable to her and may believe as follows:

1. To be loved by you, I must be perfect.
2. To be loved by you, I must make you happy.
3. To be loved by you, I must give up myself.
4. To be loved by you, I must never confront or disagree with you.
5. To be loved by you, I must never hurt you.

If I believe such things, I will expect her to appreciate me for what I'm doing and meet my unstated needs in return. I'll feel cheated and resentful when she doesn't.

Other beliefs that make intimacy impossible are these:

1. If you really know me, you won't love me.
2. Anything that goes wrong is my fault.
3. To be lovable, I must be happy all the time (and I'm not).
4. If you get close to me, I'll hurt you.
5. If we get close, you'll leave me.

Those thoughts are based on the conviction that I'm not lovable. If I believe that, I will be so ashamed of who I am that I'll be terrified of letting someone truly know me. I may run from intimacy to protect myself and then complain that I'm not loved (Victim). I may try to force people to do what I want since I know they'll never love me (Controller). Or I may try extremely hard to look lovable, even though I know I'm not (Rescuer).

Dysfunctional beliefs[3] lead to extreme behaviors. They imply we can't be our true selves and be intimate. These beliefs turn our "intimate" relationships into battlegrounds, with each person attempting to force the other into being who he or she "should" be. Sometimes these attempts to manipulate become a rigid "death grip" the partners have on each other.

To experience intimacy, we must first let go of others so they're free to be themselves. We must recognize *others are not responsible for meeting our needs.* This is very difficult, especially in marriage, where many beliefs are dysfunctional. For example, "You're my wife, so you're responsible for meeting my sexual needs. You *have to* desire me." "You're my husband, so you're responsible for meeting my emotional needs. You *must* love me." When we believe these, we turn intimacy into a task to be performed. This destroys it.

Unless my eyes are opened so I can see my partner as she really is, we can't be intimate. If I really get to know her and grant her freedom to be herself, we can develop an honest relationship.

To become capable of intimacy, I must develop a relationship with God independent of my partner. Intimacy cannot precede the discovery and development of my soul. I must face my pain, grieve my losses, develop my boundaries, and be living my own life before I can invite others in without drowning them in my emptiness.

But what happens if I'm already in a relationship based on dysfunctional beliefs? Since most of us are in such relationships, let's consider one.

JERRY AND SALLY

Jerry and Sally have been married fifteen years and have two children. Jerry has worked faithfully at his job throughout their marriage and provides a reasonably good income. Sally is working full-time now after taking a few years off when the children were young. She is a capable wife, mother and career woman. They appear to be well-adjusted in a "good" marriage raising "good" children.

Sally and Jerry are having sexual problems, however. Sally was subtly taught that sex is unmentionable and unclean *and* that she should have sex with her husband. Those are incompatible messages. She's ashamed of her sexual desires, so she's seldom aware of them. She is also ashamed when she doesn't want to have sex with her husband. Thus, if she wants sex, she feels ashamed; if she doesn't want it, she again feels ashamed.

When Jerry approaches her sexually, her shame prevents her from being responsive. But because she believes she should want to have sex with her husband, she can't just say, "No, I don't want to." Instead, she finds an escape without revealing her feelings: she has a headache or some other problem that prevents her from participating. She plays the Victim by saying, "I can't," rather than responsibly saying, "No, I don't want to."

Sally wishes Jerry didn't want sex so often so she wouldn't have to face her confusion and pain about it. She gets angry and tries to manipulate him into not wanting it by saying, "All you ever think about is sex. You're perverted!" At other times, Sally's guilt will control her, and she'll allow Jerry to have sex "because he needs it so much." Then she's rescuing him.

Jerry, too, feels ashamed. He wants to be loved by a woman but can't simply enjoy affection. He has to "score." He would never say it this way, but he feels cheated whenever they're close and don't have intercourse. A gentler, more tender part of him would enjoy just being close and touching, but he doesn't know this, because he was taught to be strong and independent. He's ashamed of any "feminine" feelings of gentleness and affection, so he's not aware of them. He's also been taught the contradictory beliefs that men are to be sexually aggressive *and* that they're bad for doing so.

Jerry feels rejected, and Sally feels used. To avoid rejection, Jerry communicates his interest in sex very carefully, trying hard to please her. Things never turn out right. Sally usually puts him off by implying that another time would be better, but somehow that better time seldom comes around. Frequently Sally will go ahead and have sex, but Jerry senses she's not really with him, so he feels unloved and undesirable. Sally is allowing herself to be used. No one is happy.

Once in a while, a crisis occurs. Out of frustration, Jerry pushes harder for sex. He tries to control by accusing Sally of being frigid and unloving. He tells her she should want to have sex with him because she's his wife. Sally responds in anger, accusing him of being oversexed and selfish. Jerry retreats feeling angry and rejected. He believes something must be wrong with him or his wife would want him. He feels ashamed. Sally feels something must be wrong with her or she would want to have sex with her husband. She also feels ashamed.

This relationship illustrates the dilemma we all face. We are bound together in damaging relationship patterns. We're also desperate for love and are our own worst enemies. As we attempt to protect ourselves from pain, we hurt our partners, who then become more defensive.

Couples often continue in this pattern for decades. After that much time, they're frequently totally estranged physically and extremely sensitive to any discussion of sex. Some have literally gone years without bringing up the subject!

How can the pattern be broken? Jerry and Sally can only begin to relate honestly if they can do so without being judged. *The paradox is that they can only learn to be intimate by having an intimate relationship.* Yet if they have an intimate relationship, they'll hurt each other. Since all of us are hurting and judge others when they're vulnerable with us, how can the cycle of pain be stopped? *Someone who can absorb the attacks and accusations and still respond in love must initiate the change.*

In the words of Scott Peck, "The healing of evil...can be accomplished only by the love of individuals. A willing sacrifice is required. The individual healer must allow his or her own soul to become the battleground. He or she must sacrificially *absorb* the evil."[4] That's what Jesus did.

> As the Father has loved me, so have I loved you. Now remain in my love. If you obey my commands, you will remain in my love....I have told you this so that my joy may be in you and that your joy may be complete. My command is this: Love each other as I have loved you. Greater love has no one than this, that one lay down his life for his friends (John 15:9-13).

Christ intervened in our cycle of mutual destruction. He was willing to love despite the pain His loving would bring. Now we are called to do the same, loving one another as Christ loved us. This means being willing to experience pain and suffering. It means seeing God in others even when they accuse and crucify us. It means saying of them as they drive in the nails, "Forgive them, for they know not what they do."

Christ took the initiative in developing an intimate friendship with us. He suffered to communicate God's love and set us free. Likewise, we are to suffer to communicate God's love to people and set them free. For Jerry and Sally to untie the knots in their relationship, they, too, will have to love as Christ did. We'll return to this after exploring sacrificial love in more detail.

THE LOVE THAT FREES

My experience as a therapist has helped me understand how love frees us. The kind of relationship and environment a therapist develops for a client is what the church is to provide for all mankind. Pastor Ray Stedman expressed this truth in a memorable analogy:

You ever feel like a frog? Frogs feel slow, low, ugly, puffy, drooped, pooped. I know—one told me. The frog feeling comes when you want to be bright but feel dumb, when you want to share but are selfish, when you want to be thankful but feel resentment, when you want to be great but are small, when you want to care but are indifferent. Yes, at one time or another each of us has found himself on a lily pad, floating down the great river of life. Frightened and disgusted, we're too froggish to budge.

Once upon a time there was a frog, only he really wasn't a frog—he was a prince who looked and felt like a frog. A wicked witch had cast a spell on him. Only the kiss of a beautiful maiden could save him. But since when do cute chicks kiss frogs? So there he sat, unkissed prince in frog form. But miracles happen. One day a beautiful maiden gathered him up and gave him a great big smack. Crash! Boom! Zap! There he was, a handsome prince. And you know the rest—they lived happily ever after.

So what is the task of the church? Kissing frogs, of course![5]

Loving as Jesus Christ loves us is akin to kissing frogs. Each of us has a real identity that the world doesn't see. We are all sons of God. We are cherished members of God's family. As Christians, we know intellectually of our new identities, yet we usually feel and behave like slaves of sin. In the words of the fairy tale, we spend most of our lives acting and feeling like frogs.

I felt like a frog last night when I responded in anger as my wife tried to help me. I feel like a frog when people are hurting and I'm too much into myself to care about them. I feel like an ugly frog when I know what's right and best but choose not to do it. I don't like myself then.

Just as the witch in the fairy tale had put a curse on the prince, trapping him in frogdom, we have the curse of sin causing us to continue in our old methods of living and hurting. The suffering love demonstrated by Jesus Christ is the "kiss" we all need to be revealed as God's children.

CHRIST'S "KISS" BRINGS PAIN

These distortions leave everybody as frogs. There are no genuine princes or princesses, because all are either denying their frogginess or trying to be comfortable in it. They want to become princes on their own terms. They want to be in control.

The fairy tale makes reality sound too simple, because it

leaves out the pain. It's going to hurt the frog when he's kissed and changes into the prince. The pain is intense when our "froggy" appearance is stripped away.

When the love of Christ reaches our souls, all the hurt, fear and shame we've denied for years well up from within and are released. The times when this transformation occurs in therapy are precious. I used to find it hard to let people sit and cry as their pain surfaced. Now I know healing is taking place.

The best analogy I've seen for this experience was written by C.S. Lewis in *The Voyage of the Dawn Treader.* The greed and self-centeredness of a young boy named Eustace turn him into a dragon. He's been most disagreeable, but now, cut off from others by his dragonlike appearance and behavior, he longs to be with people.

> He wanted to be friends. He wanted to get back among humans and talk and laugh and share things. He realized that he was a monster cut off from the whole human race. An appalling loneliness came over him....When he thought of this the poor dragon that had been Eustace lifted up its voice and wept. A powerful dragon crying its eyes out under the moon in a deserted valley is a sight and a sound hardly to be imagined.

Later Aslan the lion, the figure of Christ in the Narnia tales, appears to Eustace:

> I looked up and saw the very last thing I expected: a huge lion coming slowly towards me....I was terribly afraid of it....Well, it came closer up to me and looked straight into my eyes. And I shut my eyes tight. But that wasn't any good because it told me to follow it.

Aslan tells Eustace to undress, meaning to take off his dragon's skin. He tries unsuccessfully three times, and then he hears Aslan saying, "You will have to let me undress you." Eustace continues,

> I was afraid of his claws, I can tell you, but I was pretty nearly desperate now. So I just lay flat down on my back to let him do it....
>
> The very first tear he made was so deep that I thought it had gone right into my heart. And when he began pulling the skin off, it hurt worse than anything I've ever felt. The only thing that made me bear it was just the pleasure of feeling the stuff peel off. You know—if you've ever picked the scab of a sore place. It hurts like billy—oh but it is such fun to see it coming away....
>
> Well, he peeled the beastly stuff right off—just as I thought I'd done it myself the other three times, only they hadn't hurt....Then he caught hold of me—I didn't like that much for I was very tender underneath now that I'd no skin on—and threw me into the water. It smarted like anything but only for a moment. After that it became perfectly delicious and as soon as I started swimming and splashing I found that all the pain had gone from my arm. And then I saw why. I'd turned into a boy again.[6]

Many of us have tried to shed our frog or dragon skins repeatedly and failed. When the love of Christ penetrates as Aslan's claws did, the hurt reveals that the child within us is being recovered.

The second pain the fairy tale leaves out is what the princess must endure in kissing the frog. People don't easily accept the pain of being changed and will resist with great intensity. We deny our neediness. We try to prove we've been right about ourselves all along—that we really are frogs. If we've been used by others all our lives, we'll even try to get used by the one loving us so we can continue to avoid our deep pain.

If you've ever attempted to love a child who has been badly abused, you know how strong resistance can be to the love we need. We will fight and scream against the one who loves us, struggling to keep the control we've used for survival. We won't lay down on our backs and allow the lion to claw at our skin without putting up a terrible fight.

The princess kissing the frog has to suffer this rejection in hopes of penetrating to the prince inside. Such is the stubborn, suffering love that Jesus gives us and that we're called to give each other.

DEBBIE

To illustrate how love can change a frog into a prince or princess and how pain is part of the process, let's look at what happened with Debbie, a former client of mine. Although the therapist-client relationship is different from other intimate relationships, my experience with her will be helpful in showing how love changes lives.

When Debbie came to me, she had recently been divorced for the second time and was painfully confused about her behavior with men. She chose men who initially admired her yet hurt her, treated her disrespectfully, and would ultimately reject her. When she met someone who treated her with respect, she was cruel to him, and eventually he would reject her, too. As we discovered these patterns early in her therapy, Debbie realized what she was doing, but nothing changed. Intellectual knowledge wasn't enough.

One day she said, "I know what's best for me, but I can't do it. The harder I try, the worse I fail." Her words seemed like an echo of Paul's: "I do not understand what I do. For what I want to do I do not do, but what I hate I do" (Rom. 7:15). Debbie had genuinely committed her life to Christ, yet something inside caused her to continue to do what she didn't want to do. She was still experiencing slavery to sin, because the love of God had only begun to penetrate her soul.

Debbie had been emotionally abused by her father, so she believed she was of little value. When she accepted Christ and began to believe she could be loved, her pain started to surface. Whenever people begin to experience what they have deeply longed for and been deprived of, the pain they've carried about their loss emerges.

Because Debbie had begun to value herself, she tried to do the best things for her—to obey biblical law—but she found she could not. Her failure to live as she wanted brought her into therapy. God's love and law had prepared her for healing.

Therapy was slow with Debbie because her negative self-image was deeply ingrained. She believed, as her father had told her, that she was an ugly, messy person whom no man could love. It wasn't enough to tell her what seemed obvious to others: that she was actually a beautiful young woman who could be deeply loved.

As our relationship grew, Debbie began to phone me frequently with little regard for my circumstances. She was often belligerent. I realized she was trying to irritate me and force me to reject her as a failure.

When I refused to reject her but directly confronted her behavior instead, she became confused. She eventually stopped phoning and continued to come in, but it was very difficult, especially when I said I cared about her. She also tried other ways to force my rejection, because it was so painful for her to relate to a man who wasn't cruel.

If she wasn't being rejected by men, she expected to be used. Early in our relationship, she had behaved seductively with me, expecting that I would use her sexually. Instead, we talked about what she was doing. Her relationships with men had always begun with sexual encounters. She wanted to say no to them, but when the time came, she wanted the man's approval so much that she wouldn't refuse. She was frightened that I would be upset about what she'd been doing, but again, I didn't reprimand or threaten to quit seeing her. Rather, we discussed why she was having trouble protecting herself. She didn't need my condemnation; she was condemning herself.

After our conversations about sex, the next couple of times she fell sexually, she missed her next appointment and went days without contacting me. When she finally phoned and I welcomed her back without judgment, she was again confused. She expected rejection, and when she didn't get it, she began to feel as if her world were falling apart. This was a frightening time for Debbie. The beliefs she had lived by all her life were tumbling down. She felt out of control and uncertain about how to behave with me.

The love I communicated when she sinned was the most important love I could give. She needed the freedom to make her mistakes and still be accepted. *It was at these times that she began to realize my caring was genuine and not based on her performance.* As it dawned on her that I really did view her as valuable, she started to cry. For a number of weeks, she cried frequently. She usually had no idea why she was crying, but when we reviewed events, she'd discover that she had felt loved, and the tears followed. She was experiencing healing.

One of the most beautiful days came when she read me a passage of Scripture she had seen many times. It had come alive for her; she had realized in a new way, deep in her soul, that God loves her. She had known this intellectually for three years, but now she was feeling it. At about the same time, she began to say no to men who wanted to use her. She was putting up boundaries and developing integrity by trusting the Holy Spirit.

I describe these basic elements of therapy because they are the steps we must all go through to experience deeper levels of intimacy. Debbie was revealing herself to me because I was working to make it safe.

There are many meanings to the word "love." To love someone as Christ has commanded is to see her as a valuable creation of God and desire that she become all God has created her to be. To love Debbie, I had to:

1. believe in her as a child of God;
2. trust that the Holy Spirit was within her;
3. get to know her by hearing and understanding her emotions and experience of life;
4. be willing to withstand her attacks when she tried to resist my love;
5. resist being seduced into believing that I could fill her emptiness or meet her needs;
6. allow her the freedom to sin and still care;
7. confront her damaging behavior as inconsistent with her identity as God's child;
8. help her identify and challenge the lies she believed about herself; and
9. refuse to rescue her from pain and encourage her to mourn her losses.

I believe the work of a therapist is to see people through the eyes of Christ and offer them the love every one of us needs to become free. This creates an environment in which the steps I've described in previous chapters can occur safely. It provides a relationship in which confession is possible, in which integrity based on trusting the Spirit is encouraged, and in which the freedom to take the awkward steps toward maturity is available.

When Christ commands us to love one another, He wants us to offer this same freeing love. The church is intended to be the "therapist" for the world, for its task is kissing frogs.

PRINCESS OR FROG?

With whom have you identified in the story of the princess and the frog? Is it the poor amphibian sitting there on his lily pad, feeling ugly and wishing a beautiful princess would set him free? Perhaps you've thought. *If people would just treat me like a prince or princess, I could be one.*

When I first heard the fairy tale applied to the Christian life, I identified with the frog. I "knew" I was handsome, but nobody could see it. I was convinced that if people would just treat me right, they would see what a wonderful person I am. At times I was angry that nobody could see that or treated me "properly."

Deep inside, however, I was afraid people could see I really *was* a frog, for that's how I felt. I believed I wasn't lovable as I was and had little value. I was convinced I had to be perfect in my actions, behaviors and attitudes to be liked.

Why hadn't I identified with the princess? Why hadn't I seen myself as the person who understands the reality of the frog's identity and kisses him? As I asked this, I realized I couldn't believe anybody would want my kiss. I didn't value myself enough to realize that I could be a prince in someone's life and that my kiss could have so much power.

When I began working as a therapist, I had no idea of the power our treatment of one another has on self-image. When I first realized people were changing because I cared about them, it seemed miraculous. Why would a person enjoy being kissed by a frog like me? Did they really value *my* caring for them? Was I important and powerful enough that people's lives would change because I cared? It truly is a miracle.

Have you ever wondered how the princess would feel to see an ugly frog change into a handsome prince because of her kiss? It has to be the ultimate in self-esteem-building. That's the effect that seeing people come alive before me has had on me.

I remember when a client told me he had never been treated as a person before. My listening to him and caring about his feelings broke through his defenses and allowed him to see himself in a new way—to experience himself as God's child.

One person I especially came to value and enjoy told me she had never realized she was a person. She literally did not know she had feelings and thoughts of her own and that someone could value her for who she was.

These experiences changed me. I began to suspect I was a prince after all rather than a frog, because other frogs were turning into princes and princesses with my kiss. This wasn't occurring because I was especially gifted as a therapist but because this type of caring is what we all need to grow. Discovering the power my love had in healing others helped me believe I was a son of God. *When we love others and see the son of God begin to emerge in them as a result, we believe in our own true identity more than ever before.*

If you're feeling like a frog sitting around on your lily pad, waiting to be kissed and angry that there aren't enough kissing princesses around, maybe it's time to see yourself in a new way. Maybe *you're* the princess and the frogs are waiting for *you* to do the kissing!

We're not frogs after all. Our love for others is capable of setting them free and helping them grow. You are my prince and princess, and I'm yours.

> This is love: not that we loved God, but that he loved us and sent His Son as an atoning sacrifice for our sins. Dear friends, since God so loved us, we also ought to love one another. No one has ever seen God; but if we love each other, God lives in us and his love is made complete in us (1 John 4:10-12).

Those verses describe a principle, active in our lives, that determines whether we experience the reality of being God's children. God is saying to us in love, "This is the way life works. I want you to live with Me and experience the joy of belonging in My family. When you're loving Me and one another, you won't just be *thinking* you're children but will actually experience it. You'll see the power of love that flows through you to others and enjoy their love in return."

INTIMACY IN MARRIAGE

Let's look again at Jerry and Sally and the painful situation they're in. As long as they expect their partners to meet their needs and protect them from pain, they'll try to control each other and they'll never see the real people they married.

To become capable of intimacy, they must each face their slavery to sin and their need for recovery from its damage. They must reach the "end of their rope" and discover they can't change their partners into who they "should be" no matter how hard they try. If they can offer each other a relationship including the nine aspects of love I listed earlier, change will begin. This isn't easy. In fact, to offer love like this, they must have resources outside their relationship.

In my relationship with Debbie, I could handle her attacks, misunderstandings and resistance to change because *my self-esteem was not dependent on her behavior.* I didn't need Debbie to like me or meet my needs. If I *had* needed Debbie to do what I wanted, either to fill my needs or gain my approval as a therapist, I would have used her or tried to control her.

It's a lot easier to offer Christlike love as a therapist than as a husband or father. When I'm with my wife, I often expect her to meet my needs. I focus my unfinished and unconfessed pain and emptiness on her and, in spite of my best efforts, still try to get her to love me the way she "should." Why? Because so much of my self-esteem is wrapped up in her.

This is why Jerry and Sally will have a tough time. They're

incapable of loving the person they want to love, because they're not secure in who they are. Their attempts to love are possessive and alienating, so nothing changes.

But they don't want to let go. If they turn toward Christ for healing, it feels as if they must give up hope for the human love they desire. Jerry, for example, will have to face and grieve the reality that Sally doesn't satisfy him sexually. He can't change it, so he'll have to confront his pain. As he does this, he must develop his relationship with Christ. In turning away from Sally to meet his needs, he will be acknowledging that she is not God and will never fill his emptiness. This means ending his idolatry of Sally, setting her free, and beginning to worship the true God. Then he can begin to grow.

> *It is only by choosing Christ and leaving others free not to love us that we become our true selves and are able to give and receive love.*

To love Christ more than we love any human being, and to trust that the person He is creating in us will be loved by others, requires tremendous faith. It seems safer and easier to sacrifice our true selves, trying to gain what the world offers, than to follow Christ and trust that our deepest needs will be met in Him.

Yet, paradoxically, it is only by choosing Christ and leaving others free not to love us that we become our true selves and are able to give and receive love. Only by giving up trying to gain the world in our own way do we become able to receive it from God and look at other people with seeing eyes.

This is like receiving the "second touch" of Jesus as the blind man of Bethsaida did. Before Jesus touched his eyes the second time, people looked "like trees walking around" (Mark 8:24). After Jesus' full healing, he saw people clearly. As we recover our souls through our relationship with Christ, people look less and less like objects and more like unique people we can love. As this occurs, the joy Jesus promised begins to flow, for we are coming alive.

Jerry and Sally's intimacy will deepen as they honestly discuss their sexual difficulties with God and with each other. Trusting that everything within them can be opened up to His Spirit and that there is no condemnation in Christ will allow them to be honest.

As they grow in their ability to reveal themselves, they each must erect boundaries to protect them from the judgments and expectations of the other. While there's no condemnation in Christ Jesus, there's plenty of it in you and me. Sally must realize she does not have to meet Jerry's needs on demand by giving him sex. She must say no so she no longer gives herself away when she doesn't want to. The pain Jerry feels when she says no must be faced in his relationship with God.

Jerry must also erect boundaries by refusing to believe Sally when she accuses him of being "perverted and oversexed." He must express his desires openly and not rescue Sally from her pain by denying his sexuality. Sally will have to face her pain in her relationship with God.

They will both have much grieving to do in the process, because they're not being loved the way they want. That's not because they married a bad partner but because both of them are damaged by sin.

They've been set free, however. As they gradually explore and reveal their true feelings and desires, as they defend their true selves by saying no rather than trying to control, and as they openly say what they want, they will become intimate. Only the complete freedom of Jesus Christ makes this possible.

Being this honest will mean conflict and disappointment. But the pain will no longer have to be interpreted as evidence of unlovability. They are loved, but they aren't God. They can want whatever they want, but they won't always get it.

Clearly, progress won't go smoothly. Old patterns and pain won't disappear overnight. *They must view their growth as a lifetime process.* In the beginning, when trouble arises, they will fall back into blaming or rescuing. Gradually, as their esteem in Christ grows, they will be able to honestly discuss their problems, to share their fears and desires, and to confront one another's behavior without manipulation. They will become able to take responsibility for parts of themselves that they have disowned.

Having Jesus Christ as their source of self-esteem will empower them to absorb the attacks and rejections of their partner with less and less retaliation. Their security in Him will enable them to forgive each other, not because they "should," but because they want to. As they discuss their personal pain, the other's behavior will start to make sense. They will understand what they've triggered in the other and, because they see more clearly, forgive the other person.

To be intimate, Jerry and Sally must be willing to lay down their lives for each other. They must enter into the pain and judgment they will bring against one another so they can have the intimacy they both desire. They must "carry the cross" of commitment to one another, not by trying to eliminate pain, but by facing reality together even when it's painful.

Just as Christ was willing to suffer and die to reveal the truth about who we are, so also we must be willing to face the pain our relationships bring. In the midst of that pain, we are to communicate to others that they are sons of God. Jerry can help Sally be honest about her sexual fears and shame by making it safe for her. Sally can assist Jerry to be honest about his sexuality by allowing him to speak the uncomfortable truth.

We can be truly intimate only as we're willing to love like Christ. That means setting others free to become who they really are.[7]

OUTSIDE SUPPORT NEEDED

Jerry and Sally won't be able to develop the necessary integrity and strength by themselves. They need people outside their marriage to go to with their pain and confusion. Most people today go to pastors or therapists for this support. In recent years, more and more people are gaining their support through groups like AlAnon and Adult Children of Alcoholics. These support groups are moving beyond the focus on alcoholism that gave them their start and are beginning ministries to anyone from a dysfunctional family. As I've said, I think that's all of us.

To truly love our husbands, wives, children and parents we need a source of self-esteem outside of our families. Our relationship with Christ through the Holy Spirit within us is our most vital source of support. But just as vitally, we need the human Body of Christ. We need the living church.

Christians need to come together for the specific purpose of knowing and loving each other. We simply can't live the Christian life in isolation. It isn't enough to sit in pews and worship in the same building, as important as that is. We must obey Christ's commands to be His Body by loving each other. We'll explore this more fully in the last chapter.

FOR PERSONAL REFLECTION

1. The next time you're in a social setting, try to really see and know each of the people you encounter. Focus on them rather than on how well you're mixing. Afterward, consider these questions:

   a. How successful were you? Did you come away seeing people differently from the way you would have otherwise?

    b. What barriers did you encounter? Was it easy or difficult for you? If difficult, what was happening within you that made it hard?

    c. How did people react to you? Did they seem to sense you were behaving differently? Were you aware of any barriers they seemed to put up to make it hard for you to know them?

    d. What would it be like to live this way all the time? Could you do it? If not, why not?

2. Consider your most intimate relationships. What issues seem to cause you and your partner difficulty? Look for those that get you entangled in conversations that seem to have no resolution. Take time to review your personal history related to these issues. What hurts might you be carrying that could cause you difficulty in setting the other person free? What are your expectations? How are you trying to change them? Consider these among others: sex, money, children, in-laws, religion, roles, friends, and so on.

    How could you reach out for healing of the pain you carry that may be damaging your relationships? Think about your pain, not theirs. What do you fear about releasing the other people to be different from you? Try discussing your fears with them at a time when you're not in conflict.

FOR GROUP DISCUSSION

Sit in silence together after your opening formalities. Notice your reactions to silence. Are you comfortable with it, or do you become anxious? What makes it difficult?

    Use your entire time this way, speaking only when the Spirit leads you.

    After dismissal, you may want to discuss your reactions and

experience with others. Pay special attention to your regrets. What within you do you deeply want to share with others, but it's held in by fear or shame?

2
COMMUNITY
THE FULLNESS OF GOD'S FAMILY

*I pray...for those who will believe in
me...that all of them may be one,
Father, just as you are in me and I am
in you. May they also be in us so that
the world may believe that you have
sent me. I have given them the glory
that you gave me, that they may be one
as we are one: I in them and you in
me. May they be brought to complete
unity to let the world know that you
sent me and have loved them even as
you have loved me.*

—John 17:20-23

JESUS wants us to be one. He wants us to be united with Him, with His Father and with each other. Our complete unity is to testify to the world that God sent Jesus and that God loves us. Have we understood? I don't think so. We've been fooled by our culture into believing that we can remain isolated and still witness effectively for Christ. We can't.

I have only recently realized this. I had always felt that there was supposed to be something more to the Christian life than what I'd known. I desired the unity and love Christ describes but had only occasionally experienced it. I hadn't noticed that *my times of growth have always been intimately connected to my relationships with other Christians*. My personal study and prayer has helped me grow in *response to my relationships*, but not in isolation. If I had not been close to others and intimately shared myself, I would not have grown.

As I've noticed this and looked more closely at Scripture, I've discovered that much of the Holy Spirit's work is accomplished through Christian community. Certainly He's active in us individually, but *we won't be complete without experiencing Him as part of the whole Body of Christ*. This is much more than joining or attending a church. It means being vulnerable and becoming one with others in ways few of us have experienced.

FREE TO BE INDIVIDUALS

God doesn't force us into His family. We are free to be individuals—to feel, think and live differently from one another. He has emphasized our value as individuals by commanding us to respect each person's integrity—to not judge, use or otherwise violate others. Each of us is a free and unique child of God. American society is built on this:

> We [Americans] believe in the dignity, indeed the sacredness of the individual. Anything that would violate our right to think for ourselves, make our own decisions, live our lives as we see fit, is not only morally wrong, it is sacrilegious. Our highest and noblest aspirations, not only for ourselves, but for those we care about, for our society and for the world, are closely linked to our individualism.[1]

Because of our belief in the value of each individual, we rebelled against colonialism, abolished slavery and child labor, and enacted laws affirming equality regardless of sex, race or religion. These advances are consistent with God's love and are part of our strength as a nation. We Americans have fought against any "oneness" created by forcing the weak to give up their integrity to the strong.

Accordingly, being summoned out of our individualism into oneness is threatening. Most of the unity we've experienced has been harmful. The unity of dysfunctional families and societies is based on the destruction of people's integrity. Once we've escaped from such pain, we hesitate to risk it again. We fear exposing ourselves to situations that purport to offer family or community, because we can't be violated if we stay distant from others.

But we're paying a price for our isolation—the consequences threaten our existence. Our raped environment, fragmented families, drug problems and alienated rich and poor are symptoms of rampant individualism. We can't solve these problems on our own, and they occur because of our inability to relate.

Lonely, alienated people try to fill their emptiness through actions that damage others. The mother who abruptly leaves her family and assumes everybody will be fine does it because she "needs to be free." She's ignorant of the impact on her children. The profit-seeking executives of the chemical company dumping toxic waste don't intend to hurt others but are insensitive to them. The father who works sixty hours a week believes he's doing it for his wife and children. Because of his isolation, he's unaware of the loss they feel in his absence. If we don't recognize the heavy price we're paying for our individualism, it will destroy us.[2]

ISOLATION VERSUS THE LIFE OF CHRIST

Individualism is not Christianity. Christ has commanded us to love one another and become His family; we can't experience the life and joy Christ promised without obeying Him. We must unite together for the Holy Spirit to be active and testify to God's love for humanity. Just as Christ's obedience glorified God by revealing His true nature to the world, so our obedience will also reveal and glorify Him.

John described this clearly:

> Dear friends, let us love one another, for love comes from God. Everyone who loves has been born of God and knows God. Whoever does not love does not know God, because God is love. This is how God showed his love among us: He sent his one and only Son into the world that we might live through him. This is love: not that we loved God, but that he loved us and sent his Son as an atoning sacrifice for our sins. Dear friends, since God so loved us, we also ought to love one another. No one has ever seen God; but if we love each other, God lives in us and his love is made complete in us (1 John 4:7-12).

That last verse is astounding! The accompanying note in the

NIV Study Bible explains it well: "Since our love has its source in God's love, his love reaches full expression (is made complete) when we love fellow Christians. Thus the God 'whom no one has ever seen' is seen in those who love, because God lives in them."[3]

Our love for one another is the expression of God in this world. When we're loving one another as Christ loved, we are being His Body and revealing our Father. The glory Christ gave us from the Father is displayed to the world, and the power of the Holy Spirit is released. As we're made complete by joining together in love, we experience fullness of life and draw the world to Christ.

> *The testimony that will win the world is not our individual attractiveness as Christians but our unity and love in Christ.*

DO THEY KNOW WE'RE CHRISTIANS BY OUR LOVE?

Are our unity and love drawing all the world to Jesus Christ? When I look at the dissension between Christians and the deadness of what purports to be Christian faith, I'm tempted to conclude they are not. I want to judge the Church and accuse it of not loving as "it" should. But when I do this, I'm playing the Controller and avoiding my own responsibility.

I have not loved as Christ commanded, and I'm not alone. I'm convinced we Christians have not obeyed because we've accepted cultural definitions of love rather than those revealed by Christ. Love for us means giving things, having fun together, and being sociable and nice. It seldom includes getting to know others so well that we experience their pain and their joy.

We've also kept a safe distance from each other because it's what we're used to and because it doesn't get messy. We want God to make us better without loving as Christ does. Oswald Chambers said it like this:

> "Don't ask me to come into contact with the rugged reality of redemption on behalf of the filth of human life as it is. What I want is anything God can do for me to make me more desirable in my own eyes."
>
> To talk in [this] way is a sign that the reality of the Gospel of God has not begun to touch me....God cannot deliver me while my interest is merely in my own character.[4]

I've devoted most of my Christian life to improving my own character. I've believed Jesus wanted me to love others so that I would be a better individual. Jesus did not command us to become better people and live better lives. He commanded us to be the family of God by uniting in love and calling the world to join us. *The testimony that will win the world is not our individual attractiveness as Christians but our unity and love in Christ.* Without love we have nothing to offer.

> If I speak in the tongues of men and of angels, but have not love, I am only a resounding gong or a clanging cymbal. If I have the gift of prophecy and can fathom all mysteries and all knowledge, and if I have a faith that can move mountains, but have not love, I am nothing. If I give all I possess to the poor and surrender my body to the flames, but have not love, I gain nothing (1 Cor. 13:1-3).

No matter how gifted or successful I am as an individual, my relationships with God and others are what's eternal. My love for them and for God is what is imperishable. All the good I do as an individual is nothing if I don't have love. Even giving away everything I have and surrendering my body to flames is useless to God without love. We are called to be God's loving, unified family, and nothing less will do! It is in our experience of community, our union in love, that we will experience the risen Christ.

WHAT KIND OF LOVE?

To understand the love we're called to demonstrate, we must look again at what it means to be mature. Mature individuals use their God-given authority to take action. When negative consequences occur, our pain causes us to change direction. We grow from feeling our pain and responding to it. But what happens if our neighbors feel the pain instead of us? How do we grow then? *We don't grow unless we identify with our neighbors' pain.*

If we've been dumping our garbage over our fence each day, we'll keep doing it until we feel pain. If the neighbors dump it back plus more of their own, we'll feel pain all right, but may not realize the neighbors are dumping on us because we first dumped on them. The only way we can mature, change our behavior and grow is by knowing about our neighbors' pain as well as our own. This empathy is what's missing in our individualism and is the very essence of true Christian belief.

Because we don't identify with others' pain, society has to create laws like "It's illegal to dump your garbage on your neighbor's property." These laws are necessary because the punishments for breaking them bring pain to the violator. If I'm not aware of my neighbor's pain, I'll feel the pain of paying a fine or going to jail. This is essential, but it's not Christianity. When I do the right thing only because I fear punishment, I will be left in my loneliness, and my neighbor will be left in his. There will be no change in our hearts, for we still don't know or care about each other.

You can tell me I should care about the poor and give a portion of my income for their well-being. You can try to make me feel guilty if I don't do it, and my guilt may produce the action you desire. Fine, but don't confuse it with love. Don't believe for a moment that that's what Jesus Christ came to accomplish in me! He didn't come to point out sin by saying, "That is sin; therefore, don't do that but do this." The Pharisees and scribes tried to trap Him by asking legalistic questions, but Jesus spent very little time telling us how to change our behavior.

Instead, Jesus identified with the sinner. He took the pain, suffering and brokenness of our alienation from God upon Himself. He identified with us to communicate His love. He knows us intimately, at our weakest, at our most lonely and helpless and embraces us!

Jesus calls us to do likewise. We're no longer to worship the idols of human culture, especially American culture—idols of strength, success, prosperity and isolated individualism. Our idols are those traits that imply we're strong and don't need God or each other. In worshiping them, we ignore our incompleteness and impending death. To continue believing we're strong and complete, we must avoid identifying with the poor, the aged, the handicapped, the unborn, the ignorant and the emotionally hurting, for they will remind us of our own weakness and mortality.

Jesus calls us to identify with our neighbors by joining Him on the cross. There Jesus experienced our death, loneliness and shame. There He became one with us. And only there can we become one with Him.

> Your attitude should be the same as that of Christ Jesus: Who, being in very nature God, did not consider equality with God something to be grasped, but made himself nothing, taking the very nature of a servant, being made in human likeness. And being found in appearance as a man,

he humbled himself and became obedient to death—even death on a cross! (Phil. 2:5-8).

We won't need rules telling us how to act if we humble ourselves and identify with the weak and hurting. When we see and feel our brokenness, our false, manipulative images will be destroyed, and we'll become capable of loving.

We won't have to be told to love powerless minorities, for we will be one with them. When we identify with the confusion and fear of the young girl considering an abortion, we won't have to be told to care about her for we will be one with her. Our actions in responding to her may differ, but our motives will be one; we will be obeying Christ by loving her. In Christian community, new answers and actions will be discovered and come to life.

> Therefore, I urge you, brothers, in view of God's mercy, to offer your bodies as living sacrifices, holy and pleasing to God—which is your spiritual worship....For by the grace given me I say to every one of you: Do not think of yourself more highly than you ought, but rather think of yourself with sober judgment, in accordance with the measure of faith God has given you. Just as each of us has one body with many members, and these members do not all have the same function, so in Christ we who are many form one body, and each member belongs to all the others....Be devoted to one another in brotherly love. Honor one another above yourselves....Share with God's people who are in need. Practice hospitality....Rejoice with those who rejoice; mourn with those who mourn. Live in harmony with one another. Do not be proud, but be willing to associate with people of low position (Rom. 12:1,3-5,10,13,15-16).

Paul called us to obey the Lord by leaving our self-sufficient individualism and joining His family. To reveal God to the world and experience the joy God intends for us, we must develop true Christian community.

WHAT IS CHRISTIAN COMMUNITY?

In his book *The Different Drum,* Scott Peck describes community as follows:

> A group of individuals who have learned how to communicate honestly with each other, whose relationships go deeper than their masks of composure, and who have developed some significant commitment to "rejoice together, mourn together," and to "delight in each other, make others' conditions our own."[5]

Community occurs when people are able to drop their masks and reveal their true selves to each other. They work to identify with one another's sorrows and joys and to enter into honest, loving relationships.

Peck describes many characteristics of community that he has discovered and experienced. A crucial one is safety. "Once a group has achieved community, the single most common thing members express is: 'I feel safe here.'"[6] Grace and forgiveness predominate, so we are free and secure enough to reveal ourselves.

Another necessary element of community is the confession of brokenness—revealing to one another how we're hurting and incomplete. People in community identify with one another's pain. They don't try to fix or convert each other but come alongside the hurting. They make it their goal to become one with them.

This is what we are commanded to do as Christians. And when we do it, we're promised the blessings and power of the

Holy Spirit. For Christians, "the work of community building is seen as preparation for the descent of the Holy Spirit. The spirit of community is a manifestation of the Holy Spirit."[7]

When I first read *The Different Drum*, I was skeptical. I recognized immediately that what Peck describes is what I have always wanted the Christian church to be. I desperately hoped he was right—that it's possible to develop true community. Since that time, I have participated in two Community Building Workshops based on Peck's perspective.

I've learned a lot in these workshops. (For more information about such workshops, see "Resources for Community Development" at the end of this chapter.) I discovered that the biggest barrier to my experiencing community is me. I discovered I want people to love according to my rules and to meet my standards. I discovered ways I try to be God that were invisible before I committed myself to becoming intimate with a group of people. I realized just how difficult it is to obey Jesus' command not to judge others.

> Do not judge, and you will not be judged. Do not condemn, and you will not be condemned. Forgive, and you will be forgiven. Give, and it will be given to you. A good measure, pressed down, shaken together and running over, will be poured into your lap. For with the measure you use, it will be measured to you (Luke 6:37,38).

Being in community revealed the "measure" I was using more clearly than I had seen before. I realized how judgmental and condemning I was in spite of my good facade.

Yet even as I was discovering these painful things about myself, I was experiencing love. Committing myself to love a group of people and honestly reveal myself brought unexpected growth and blessings. I received healing in areas of my life that have haunted me for years.

Participating in community also helped me love in new ways. I remember reacting negatively to certain individuals when our workshops began. At the end of our weekend together, I realized I was not unlike them at all. I could identify with, accept and care about people I would have had great difficulty with before.

My workshop experiences have convinced me that the most important aspect of what it means to be the Body of Christ has been neglected. We have not emphasized loving one another in obedience to Christ's command adequately, so we've experienced little of His loving, empowering family. We're passing each other on Sunday mornings, hurting and longing for love but too afraid to tell each other about it. *We've been too afraid and proud to obey Jesus.*

Although we experience some community in the midst of our isolation, God intends that being His family should be the church's highest priority. We've only given it lip service. As a result, we're missing the essence of what it means to be God's people. We're not experiencing His power and presence as we could when we gather together in His name: "Again, I tell you that if two of you on earth agree about anything you ask for, it will be done for you by my Father in heaven. For where two or three come together in my name, there am I with them" (Matt. 18:19,20).

We've misunderstood Christ by believing that gathering in formal worship and prayer is all we need to experience His power. Not so! His command was to love one another. Sitting isolated in pews without opening our hearts omits knowing and loving each other! Our pretense at unity is powerless. As we draw close to each other to become intimate with Christ and with each other, *then we'll have His power.*

Are there churches doing this? Yes. One that I'm familiar with is the Church of the Saviour in Washington, D.C. A group of Christians led by Gordon Cosby founded the church in 1946.

Consider some of the convictions of the church as revealed in the writings of Elizabeth O'Connor.

> [In committing oneself to the church,] one has become a part of a people with whom the whole of life is bound—a fellowship where all the members are necessary to one another as the eye is to the hand, and as close as, and more intimate than, the members of a family. This is what will mark the church as different. This is what a spiritually starved world will wonder at: "See how they love one another." We are members now of that family of faith with ties deeper than any we have known before.[8]

After visiting this church and speaking to its members, I left convicted that I had seen the way the Body of Christ is intended to function. Being in real community as they are includes difficulties and conflict. Their honest self-appraisal made that clear. But Christ has not called us to develop a utopia for Him. We can't in a sin-damaged world. He has called us to be His sacrificial Body.

COMMUNITY CANNOT BE OUR GOAL

There are dangers in setting out to develop community. One is that we must not make community itself the goal. Community is possible only if it develops from pursuing a purpose greater than that of being community.

This is similar to what I tell couples in premarital counselling: People who are committed to marriage seldom have good marriages. Marriage itself cannot be our goal. We must commit ourselves to loving our spouses rather than to having a good marriage. Love creates a marriage.

In the same way our goal must be to respond to Christ's love by obeying His commands. Our commitment is not to community but to love the people we're with. Gordon Cosby says it this way:

> [Our commitment] says to a specific group of people that I am willing to be with you. I am willing to belong to you, I am willing to be the people of God with you. This is never a tentative commitment that I can withdraw from. It is a commitment to a group of miserable, faltering sinners who make with me a covenant to live in depth until we see in each other the mystery of Christ himself and until in these relationships we come to know ourselves as belonging to the Body of Christ.[9]

Our commitment is to the people; our intention is to be Christ's Body.

CHRISTIAN COMMUNITY, THE FUNCTIONAL FAMILY

Earlier, I defined the dysfunctional family as one that hinders us from becoming who God created us to be. When we commit ourselves to becoming one in Christ, we are setting out to become God's functional family. Christian community is committed to helping all members become who God created them to be. Every characteristic of the dysfunctional family finds its opposite in God's family.

God's family acknowledges need. Dysfunctional families are ashamed of and hide their needs. God's family reveals needs; it's what draws them together! Speaking of our hunger for love reveals our common humanity and interdependence. Our experience of His family will begin when those of us who hunger after God and meaning for our lives are bold enough to reveal it. As long as we pretend to be self-sufficient in our isolation, God's family will not exist.

God's family lives in the light. Dysfunctional families keep emotions, needs and conflict in darkness. Christian community knows that healing and forgiveness can only be experienced through honest confession. By confessing its blindness, God's family steps into His light. Members are committed to remaining in His light and trusting His healing power, so they're not surprised when we're froggy rather than princelike. They will be less likely to be surprised at or to judge our sinfulness, because they will be sharing their own. Because the "death" of confession is encouraged, the joy of resurrection is experienced.

Twelve-step groups such as Alcoholics Anonymous are excellent examples of how confession can be an integral part of community. Members enter the fellowship by confessing weakness and need: "I'm Larry, and I'm an alcoholic." Christian community will be characterized by people gathering together and honestly confessing, "I'm Ken, and I'm a sinner saved only by God's grace."

God's family trusts the integrity of each person. Dysfunctional families develop the appearance of unity by suppressing and destroying integrity. God's family believes each individual's personality is needed for its wholeness. It encourages the expression of personal integrity and trusts the Holy Spirit to create the unity.

Trusting each person's integrity gives individuals the freedom to say no. Members can remain silent in community if they desire. It is assumed that when their boundaries are developed and they realize deep in their souls that they're free to be themselves, the Spirit will motivate their participation.

God's family encourages the expression of each member's gifts. Dysfunctional families force gifts and talents to be buried. God's family encourages the expression of dreams and desires. The family trusts the Holy Spirit to be active in each person and God's creativity and life to emerge from them. Christian community knows each one has gifts granted by the Spirit, and it looks actively for them.

When someone is guided by the Spirit to a particular service, others in the family will prayerfully consider joining them. They know they are free not to participate. If they do join in, their involvement will be wholehearted.

I like the way Gordon Cosby has emphasized the respect God's family is to have for the integrity of each person and his or her gifts:

> We are not sent into the world in order to make people good. We are not sent to encourage them to do their duty. The reason people have resisted the Gospel is that we have gone out to make people good, to help them do their duty, to impose new burdens on them, rather than calling forth the gift which is the essence of the person himself.
>
> They can be what in their deepest hearts they know that they were intended to be, they can do what they were meant to do. As Christians we are heralds of these good tidings.
>
> How do we do this? We begin by exercising our own gifts. The person who is having the time of his life doing what he is doing has a way of calling forth the deeps of another. Such a person is good news. He is the embodiment of the freedom of the new humanity. The person who exercises his own gift in freedom can allow the Holy Spirit to do in others what He wants to do.[10]

God's family encourages the maturing of each individual. Dysfunctional families do not allow mistakes. God's family encourages bold actions and helps people learn from mistakes. Members are encouraged to use their authority and take responsibility for the consequences.

The family of God will not rescue us from the consequences of our actions unless we're truly helpless and their intervention is an act of love. It is assumed that all must carry their own burdens, but also that burdens are to be shared. Knowing when to help friends carry burdens and when to let them go it alone for their growth can be difficult. This is worked out in each relationship with the guidance of the Holy Spirit.

When family members behave in ways contradictory to their identity as sons of God, they are confronted in love. Such confrontations are not done hastily or by isolated individuals but by the community. People don't tell others what to do; they hear them and work to understand.

God's family assumes conflicts will occur between people because they're different. It views this conflict as opportunity for growth. Dysfunctional families avoid conflict and assume that it means somebody is wrong and bad. God's family knows each person has been created differently and that the Body of Christ needs every person's input. Conflict is viewed as opportunity for the Holy Spirit to heal and speak. It's assumed that no one individual speaks for God but that the Body, united in love, reveals God's will. Every individual is encouraged to speak, because open expression of pain brings life, while unexpressed conflict and pain destroy it.

> In this strange community where commitment is not tentative we become free to act and to speak. We can take risks that we could not take in other situations, which include the risk of getting in touch with our own unfelt feelings....We can choose to express anger and therefore keep the sun from setting on it. We can take the risk of telling a brother what stands between us, if we know there will be another time when we are together, and that it does not depend on what does or does not happen in this moment.[11]

Members of God's family share a common concern for the health of the family. "Protecting the family" in dysfunctional families means protecting its image and keeping secrets. Caring for the family of God is demonstrated by continued personal and group confession and honest discussion of anything that threatens family unity. The boundaries of the family are protected by keeping the confession and pain of members confidential rather than exposing them to the world's judgment. But within the family, openness prevails.

Family members also demonstrate their concern by considering the effect their behavior will have on the Christian community. They don't think of themselves as individuals only, but also as members of the Body of Christ.

So whether you eat or drink or whatever you do, do it all for the glory of God. Do not cause anyone to stumble, whether Jews, Greeks or the church of God—even as I try to please everybody in every way. For I am not seeking my own good but the good of many, so that they may be saved (1 Cor. 10:31-33).

God's family is devoted to sacrificial love for all humanity. The emptiness of the dysfunctional family has nothing to offer the world. The people of God discover a power in their fellowship that they are willing to give to others. The development of individual integrity enables members to give sacrificially, not out of obligation, but as an expression of love.

There is no unity with Christ or his people unless we serve. This is why the exercising of gifts is important. It enables us to serve, to give of ourselves to another. This is how we find out what oneness in Christ is about. When you are moving out in faith to serve another, there comes a oneness within. It makes of your words unifying words and of your deed a unifying deed. There is no Christian community not rooted in service and no Christian service not rooted in relationship. It is the feet of His friends that Christ washes.[12]

Experiencing this love prepares us to reach out to those outside the community. For days after my last Community Building Workshop, I was more aware, open and caring toward the people I encountered than I had ever been. I made friends wherever I went. My heart was tender, sensitive and vulnerable. I didn't *try* to do this; it was a natural part of who I was. When we're loving and being loved, we will have much to offer the hurting world around us. We'll be prepared to be broken bread and poured-out wine for others.

> *Community doesn't just happen because we've decided to do it. It's the product of committing ourselves to each other and working through the conflicts and troubles that arise.*

God's family gives us permission to be children. Dysfunctional families often have difficulty allowing play. God's family has a sense of humor and a desire for fun. It's a safe place to be a child. This is incredibly difficult for many of us. But the safety of a loving family gradually releases the playfulness and joy in each of us. It's unbelievably freeing to express this.

God's family is physically demonstrative and affectionate. Dysfunctional families are deathly afraid of sexuality. God's family knows sex is a gift of God and is able to discuss it openly and enjoy its warmth. This honesty about sex entails risk and is probably the most difficult growth area for most of us. The miracle is that *when we begin to be open about it, we can handle it responsibly.* Our shame and fear keep it hidden and difficult to express and control.

The child in each of us wants to be hugged and touched. We don't have to have intercourse with others to express our love for them. Our commitment to restrict intercourse to marriage will be much more secure when we can own and express our sexuality in its fullness.

God's family treats us as sons and daughters of God. Dysfunctional families shame, accuse and use us. God's family witnesses to His power by committing itself to being the family we have longed for since birth, a family that sees us through the affirming, loving eyes of God. God's family knows of our true identity in Jesus Christ and looks for Him to be revealed in us.

IS THIS POSSIBLE?

A realistic response to my description of God's family is "Who are you kidding? This is impossible!" In human terms, it *is* impossible. We're incapable of it. And Parker Palmer says we must begin right there.

> When we first come into community, we are blissfully ignorant of just how agonizing it is. We come with high expectations: Where the world hates, community loves: where the world wounds, community heals: where the world betrays, community trusts. Indeed, our expectations for life together take the form of a tacit, unconscious theology that pins our hopes for wholeness on community itself. I have come to call this a theology of "salvation by interaction." Somehow we believe that if we look deeply enough into each other's eyes, talk honestly and openly enough, resolve our conflicts and celebrate our joys, we will be saved.
>
> The only problem with this theology is that it doesn't work. After an initial period of euphoria, we discover that there is as much hatred and wounding and betrayal in community as in the world. I have lived in an intentional spiritual community for eleven years, and I still hold to an axiom I formulated after only a year of life together: "Community is that place where the person you least want to live with always lives." I also hold to the corollary I formulated

two years later, "And when that person moves away, someone else arrives immediately to take his or her place."

Community life, like marriage, usually begins with romance. But when the romance fades, as it must, community becomes a labor of love requiring simple tenacity.[13]

The romantic stage is what Scott Peck calls pseudocommunity. We come together anticipating a wonderful, life-changing experience. We are going to love each other, heal each other, and save the world. So we work at being polite, caring and nice rather than revealing anything that might be risky or frightening. We fake community.

Pseudocommunity is all most of us have known. Much of what we experience in church is pseudocommunity. There's no growth, life or Spirit in it. Pseudocommunity's lack of fruit reveals its falseness.

Yet pseudocommunity is where we must begin, because we have *reason* to be afraid. We fear being vulnerable because this is a dangerous world. Community doesn't just happen because we've decided to do it. It's the product of committing ourselves to each other and working through the conflicts and troubles that arise. Just as our individual growth is a process, so community develops gradually and in stages.

When the romance and pretense of pseudocommunity fade, we enter the stage of development Peck calls "chaos." During this stage, the three faces of sin are visible. People are controlling, rescuing or playing Victim. Everybody is trying to heal or convert everybody else, and confusion reigns. We seldom experience this for long in everyday living, because we run from it. In church, we're usually so busy being nice and have so little at stake in being together that we seldom get close enough to encounter it.

All too often, when chaos *does* occur in church communities, rather than remaining together and working through it, we split.

Figure 19

Our commitment to others disappears when we can't control or fix them. Our dreams of love and community die when we have to love real people. We are very much like Linus (see fig. 19).

We can envision ourselves as loving, unified members of God's family when we keep it in the abstract and imagine ourselves loving mankind. But loving real people is the most difficult thing in the world.

After expressing his skepticism about "salvation by interaction," Parker Palmer states his conviction that the major function of community is disillusionment.

> The primary spiritual function of community is to disillusion us about each other and about ourselves, remembering that "disillusionment" is a positive process in the spiritual life. It means losing our illusions so that we may come closer to reality. The human failures of community teach us to put our trust in God, where it belongs, and not in our own skills and charm. As we learn this lesson, the paradox ripens. In trusting God we become more trustworthy to each other, more available for the authentic community that is grounded in God's power and not our own.[14]

Just as an individual must reach the point of despair to turn to God for healing, so also must communities. We have to experience our inability to love and give up attempting it in our own power so God can empower us.

To be God's family, we must stay through the chaos, experience the disillusionment, and remain committed. Scott Peck calls this third stage "emptying." Members of the group confess and let go of their attempts to control and their preconceptions of what community should be. Only then do the closeness and love that mark true community occur.

Community is a work of the Holy Spirit. We will recognize it by the absence of judgment and a deep sense of peace.

There will be a great deal of sadness and grief expressed; but there will also be much laughter and joy. There will be tears in abundance. Sometimes they will be tears of sadness, sometimes of joy. Sometimes, simultaneously, they will be tears of both. And then something almost more singular happens. An extraordinary amount of healing and converting begins to occur—now that no one is trying to convert or heal. And community has been born.[15]

The precious times when we're aware of the presence of the Holy Spirit in our midst are tastes of heaven. For a while we know the reality of being God's children. We realize we really are one in Christ and secure in His love. We experience the glory of God.

Community is a gift. We can't make it happen whenever we want, so we won't always experience joy when we're together. At times we will retreat into pseudocommunity; at other times, chaos will reign. But even when we don't experience the closeness of those special moments of joy, we will be loving one another by obeying Christ, and the life that flows from our love will reveal the true God and His grace.

The Christian Church has a secret at her heart and the only call upon her is to share it. Whenever by repentance and forgiveness one enters into the community of grace, he discovers the very end of life. Another person is then the possessor of the news that must be told, and must run to find a housetop from which to proclaim it.[16]

Two Views of Community

Parker Palmer believes the primary function of community is disillusionment. In contrast, Scott Peck begins *The Different Drum* by writing, "In and through community lies the salvation of the world."[17] He sees community as necessary to the spiritual healing we all need. The seemingly contradictory positions of these men reveal two important elements of community. They are both essential for our growth in Christ.

Undergirding the truth in the two positions are the two commandments given by Jesus: "Jesus replied: 'Love the Lord your God with all your heart and with all your soul and with all your mind.' This is the first and greatest commandment. And the second is like it: 'Love your neighbor as yourself.' All the Law and the Prophets hang on these two commandments" (Matt. 22:37-40).

> *Obeying Christ's first command motivates us to obey His second.*

When we focus on our individual relationship with God, He loves, heals and empowers us through the work of His Spirit in our hearts. Yet if we try to "put up a shelter" and stay there, as Peter wanted to do when the Lord was transfigured, we will become stagnant and lifeless. In our individual communion with Him, God reveals our need for others and commands us to go out and love them. Obeying Christ's first command motivates us to obey His second.

When we obediently love the family of God, we experience healing, but also injury and conflict. We are both affirmed as sons of God and deeply disillusioned by our failure to be community. The disillusionment is to drive us back into our individual, internal relationship with God. It keeps us from making community an idol. Community is the human expression of God, not God Himself. It is not self-sustaining but dependent on Him. Obeying the second command points us back to the first, to love the Lord our God.

I have experienced both the healing power of community described by Scott Peck and the disillusionment of Palmer. I need them both. The Holy Spirit is both within me and within my community.

If I decide to limit my spiritual communion to confession and conversation with the Spirit, my growth will be real but limited. I am not the whole Body of Christ, only one hand or foot. I need your gifts and abilities to be whole. I'm lonely and unfulfilled without you. A well-developed foot without the rest of the body is useless.

At the same time, if I focus completely on my relationship with the community and neglect my inner journey, I'll become frustrated and disillusioned. I will experience some growth by listening to the Spirit revealed in the church, but my participation will soon wither. I won't be a very good foot. Eventually my unfinished personal growth will prevent me from loving you as God intends. I will have little to offer if I neglect my own soul.

Jesus gave two specific commands because we need them both. We are to love God with all our hearts and minds *and* love each other as Christ loves us. I discovered a rhythm between these in my most recent experience of community (see fig. 20).

OUR NEED FOR GOD AND HIS PEOPLE

Our group had been together for two days. Many members of the group were confessing personal barriers to community. They were "emptying." After one person's sharing, a warm and exciting sense of peace came over me. I felt safe and loved and joyful. I wondered if others could see that I was crying. Community was beginning for me.

Then a member of the group said something that pushed a button I didn't know I had. What he said seemed pleasant and innocent to most. It seemed very "nice." But everyone's sharing had been deep and personal for some time, and this niceness struck a chord deep within me. I became angry, because his niceness seemed like pretense. I couldn't accept it as genuine.

THE RHYTHM IN OUR RELATIONSHIPS WITH GOD AND HIS FAMILY

Movement into our relationship with God is motivated by our disillusionment with the world, our desire for individual wholeness, and obedience to the Holy Spirit.

Movement into God's family is motivated by our need for others, our desire for corporate wholeness, and obedience to the Holy Spirit.

OUR INDIVIDUAL
RELATIONSHIP
WITH GOD

OUR RELATIONSHIP
WITH GOD'S
FAMILY

"Love the Lord Your
God."

"Love one another as
I have loved you."

Being one with
the Father

Being one with
the Son

Figure 20

I told at the beginning of chapter 8 how my controlling reactions then robbed me of my joy. But there's more to the story.

That night, I felt deeply disappointed and frustrated about the group. We hadn't really become as close as I had hoped. We didn't seem united or loving. I felt the disillusionment Parker Palmer describes. I described my frustration and irritation to my wife by phone, and she asked a simple question: "What would be wrong with letting people be nice if they want to be?"

> *When we develop a rhythm between our personal spiritual lives and loving in community, we will grow.*

The question revealed unfinished business in me. Why couldn't I release others to God rather than controlling? Then I understood it wasn't the other person's niceness I was angry about but my own. I've often presented a false but pleasant front when I actually felt angry or upset, and my anger at my own pretense had spilled out into the group.

That night, as a result of conflict in community, I saw and confessed sin in myself. A new part of me entered God's kingdom. Without the intense interactions and conflict in the group, I would have remained blind. Being in community had forced me to see the plank in my own eye: "Why do you look at the speck of sawdust in your brother's eye and pay no attention to the plank in your own eye? How can you say to your brother, 'Brother, let me take the speck out of your eye, when you yourself fail to see the plank in your own eye?'" (Luke 6:41,42).

The next day, I confessed what I had realized to the group. The person I had hurt responded by forgiving and loving me. My experience of closeness and community returned. The love was healing.

As my experience reveals, when we develop a rhythm

between our personal spiritual lives and loving in community, we will grow. The feelings we discover in prayer can be brought into community for exploration and understanding. The conflicts and issues revealed in community can be presented to God in our times of meditation. If we attempt to make either our sole source of life, we will stagnate. We need to move back and forth between the two areas regularly.

COMMUNITY REVEALS UNFINISHED CHILDHOOD PAIN

That one person in community whom Palmer describes as "the person you least want to live with" usually represents a part of you that you've disowned. Aggressive, pushy people have been hard for me to love. Having been raised to be "good," I've disowned much of my aggressiveness and strength. I'm not supposed to say or do things to upset people. I discovered in community that the people who most disturbed me usually knew what they wanted and said it. I had projected disowned parts of myself onto them. I couldn't accept their aggressiveness because I was not supposed to be aggressive.

These projections of our disowned parts obviously block community. But we can discover our projections and disowned parts by interacting closely with different kinds of people. *The very conflicts that make community difficult are the reason God wants us together!* I needed the niceness as well as the aggressiveness of others to acknowledge my projections. By confessing my pretense and accepting aggressive feelings in myself, I became more whole. Because of this new wholeness, I could give love to and receive it from people I had felt alienated from before.

Elizabeth O'Connor describes how this healing can occur in *Journey Inward, Journey Outward:*

In the Church of the Saviour we live in community, and

you cannot live in community and hide your problems. In fact, community will bring into light problems which, though they are yours, are often hidden even from you. Relationships in depth will always do that. Christian community probably comes the closest of any community to the family of our childhood, and the unassimilated hurts and unresolved problems of that family come to light again in the context of the new "family of faith." Sometimes apparently well-adjusted persons come into the life of the church, people of action, ready to get on with the mission of the church, and then a few months or a year later things do not appear to be as well with them. They are actually much better off, because a lot of their activity had been motivated by anxiety of one kind or another, or simply the need to belong. Others are afraid of relationship in depth and discover that, while they yearn for community, they back away when people get too close. Still others find stirring in them yearnings that had been quieted and are now raised to life by the life around. The reasons are different for each person, but the experience is always pain. No real growth takes place without pain. Nothing is born into the consciousness without suffering.[18]

This kind of growth and healing simply cannot take place in isolation. God's family is to be the place where we can reveal our frogginess and still be loved. Our dysfunctional patterns can be recognized for what they are with less chance of our being judged. This can happen because everybody is acknowledging weakness and damaging behavior.

Entering God's family is a decision to face reality both in ourselves and in those to whom we commit ourselves. Members of God's family are prepared to sacrifice themselves for one another's well-being and growth, knowing that this will include conflict, disagreement and pain. Yet we freely make this commitment because Christ commanded it.

CALLED TO BE GOD'S FAMILY

In the last chapter, I said we must have a source of self-esteem and power outside our relationships to be able to love people as Christ loved. Jerry and Sally, the couple with a troubled sexual relationship, need support from outside their marriage so they can love one another sacrificially. All parents need support outside their natural families so they can love their children even while they're learning to love themselves.

Many of the people I have worked with in therapy are Christians active in their churches. Usually when I ask if they have someone they can share their pain with outside therapy, they answer no. They are worshiping, attending Sunday School classes, and participating on committees. But when they need someone to reveal their souls to, there's no one. They have no genuine community.

Thus, I'm afraid we in the church are not experiencing the power of being sons of God because we, too, are behaving as a dysfunctional family. Most of the organized church is following the rules "Don't talk, don't trust, and don't feel." We have hidden our pain and need in the darkness and avoided the light, even as we sit in our pews and worship the One we're avoiding.

If we aren't experiencing God's family, let's be honest about it. I've often heard pastors exhort their congregations to witness about Christ to their friends and neighbors. Before doing this, however, we should ask one important question: "Have I received anything to witness to?" If we speak of Christ to others without having received anything real from Him, our emptiness speaks louder than our words and there is no attractiveness to what we offer. If we have not received what's been promised, we must acknowledge our emptiness for it to be filled.

I know what I've said in this chapter brings up many questions. We know so little about living in community and being the family God desires us to be. As we obey the Spirit and reach out to each others in love, we'll make lots of mistakes and hurt people along the way. We can't avoid the mistakes, but we pay a bigger price by not risking them. We must join together in obedience to our Lord. His sacrifice has set us free to act boldly.

Taking Christ's command to love one another seriously will threaten the institutional church. Many of its programs and structures actually destroy community rather than encourage it. But our highest priority must be obeying God and becoming His family. This will mean finding new forms unique to our culture that encourage community to develop.

> The structures of the Church have little to do with the need of the world. That is half the problem. The other half is that they so often have little to do with the need of those within the church. They do not help us to realize our essential selves—to follow Christ, who saves us from being other than who we are. The church has too often told us what to do and failed to help us become who we can be. The new forms of the Church will be shaped by the need of every man to become the person he can become. It is our common humanity that we affirm, our need of one another, and above all our sonship—we are joint heirs with Christ. It is the glorious freedom of the sons of God to which all men are called that our structures are to proclaim.[19]

CONCLUSION

I know the family of God as I've described it sounds incredibly idealistic. Many of you will conclude that people can't love in the ways I've described. I understand how you feel. I, too, become discouraged and resign myself to just living my life like everybody else. I decide to settle for less than my spirit yearns for and dismiss my dreams as unrealistic. But when I do that, I begin to die.

Is it idealistic to believe that Jesus meant it when He commanded us to love one another? Was He unrealistic when He asked the Father to make us one with each other and with Him? When we say that committing ourselves to becoming genuine Christian community is impractical, we're revealing our lack of faith, not our pragmatism.

You have been created to be a special part of the Body of Christ. Until you discover and express yourself in the way you desire, you will remain frustrated and unfulfilled. All the possessions and pleasures of life will leave you empty until you pursue your God-given self. He has set us free to be who we are and to learn from our mistakes. By setting us free, He has taken away all our excuses. Deep in your heart, if there's something you want more than anything else, you now have no excuse for not pursuing it.

To discover your dream, you need God's family! That's true because you have been created to fulfill a special function in that family. If you don't give up everything else in this world for the "pearl of great price," you will always carry an emptiness within. Only in God's family will we be fulfilled.

We hesitate to obey Christ, because once again we have believed Satan's lies. It is the voice of evil that tells us loving community is impossible. It's Satan's voice that says this is impossibly idealistic and we should resign ourselves to "reality." *Reality is Jesus Christ.* Anything that pretends to be real but discounts or destroys our dreams in Christ is false and must be challenged. *We not only* can *become God's family through the power of the Holy Spirit, but we must become His family.* There is nothing more urgent or necessary in all of life.

We must consciously and purposefully decide whom we are going to believe. The Bible says Christ has set us free, has empowered us, and we can be His people. If that's not true, it's time we faced it and quit playing games. But if we believe Jesus, we must obey Him, love one another, and unite as His people. To do this, we must be willing to face our pain, share it with each other, and trust the Holy Spirit to perform miracles we cannot anticipate.

My prayer for you is that which Paul offered for the Ephesian church:

> I kneel before the Father, from whom his whole family in heaven and on earth derives its name. I pray that out of his glorious riches he may strengthen you with power through his Spirit in your inner being, so that Christ may dwell in your hearts through faith. And I pray that you, being rooted and established in love, may have power, together with all the saints, to grasp how wide and long and high and deep is the love of Christ, and to know this love that surpasses knowledge—that you may be filled to the measure of all the fullness of God (Eph. 3:14-19).

FOR PERSONAL REFLECTION

1. Consider these verses:

> As the Father has loved me, so have I loved you. Now remain in my love. If you obey my commands, you will remain in my love, just as I have obeyed my Father's commands and remain in his love. I have told you this so that my joy may be in you and that your joy may be complete (John 15:9-11).

Do you know the joy Christ was describing? Have you had those times when His joy filled you and you knew its reality? If you have not, I encourage you to talk to God about it.

If you're aware of a hunger for His joy, confess it to Him and ask Him to help you get to know Him and His family so intimately that His joy becomes yours. He may guide you to particular people or into situations that will open doors for you. I encourage you not to be become disheartened, for I've been there, too. He is faithful, and He will work to draw you close to Him. The joy He promises is real and can be experienced by becoming part of His loving family. If you haven't discovered His family yet, keep looking. He will reward your search.

2. If you *have* experienced His joy, take time to remember those special events and situations in which His Spirit was most evident. Consider the circumstances when you've known His joy. Were you in community with other Christians at that time? Were you being especially vulnerable with someone? As you review those special times, ask the Lord to reveal any truths He would like you to carry with you and act upon. Especially consider your role in His family.

3. Are there ways in which you *want* to obey Him but you've hesitated to do so? Take them before Him in prayer, and listen for His direction.

FOR GROUP DISCUSSION

As you meet together, discuss those special times in your life when you have been in community—when you *knew* you were experiencing God's family. As you share those times with each other, listen to His Spirit within you for truths He wants you to express and remember.

If any members of your group have not experienced joy, pray together (if they desire to) for God to reveal Himself in a new and deeper way. Remember, we can't make joy our goal. It will come only as a result of getting to know Christ and receiving His love. If we haven't experienced the love and joy Christ promised, it doesn't mean there's something bad about us. It just means there's a whole lot more love available than we've been able to receive so far. Our goal must be to know Christ and His people more intimately. The joy, when it comes, is an unexpected blessing.

RESOURCES FOR COMMUNITY DEVELOPMENT

If you'd like to know more about Christian community, write or call:

Wellspring—Church of the Saviour
11411 Neelsville Ch. Rd.
Germantown, MD 20874
(301) 428-3373

If you ask to be put on their mailing list, you will receive their regular newsletter containing information about retreats, books and educational opportunities related to Christian community and servanthood. I highly recommend attending an orientation retreat at their Wellspring retreat center.

A second source of information about community development (not exclusively Christian) is:

The Foundation for Community Encouragement Inc.
7616 Gleason Road
Knoxville, TN 37919
(615) 690-4334

The Foundation will also send a newsletter. It gives dates and locations for Community Building Workshops throughout the United States. They also offer Community Building Skills Seminars in Knoxville on a regular basis.

The Foundation has speakers available and offers help to churches that desire to deepen their experience of community.

NOTES

Chapter 1

1. W. E. Vine, *Vine's Expository Dictionary of Old and New Testament Words* (Old Tappan, N.J.: Revell, 1981), vol. 4, p. 54.
2. Ibid., vol. 2, p. 207.
3. Alice Miller, *The Drama of the Gifted Child* (New York: Basic Books, 1981), p. 5.
4. Ibid., p. 7.
5. I want to thank Dr. Everett Shostrom for developing the exercises upon which these are based.

Chapter 2

1. M. Scott Peck, *People of the Lie* (New York: Simon & Schuster, 1983), p. 206.
2. C. S. Lewis, *The Problem of Pain* (New York: Macmillan, 1962), p. 110.
3. Analogies can be useful in helping us understand, but they always have weaknesses. I am using this one to focus on our need for God, the results of our separation from Him and God's response. This analogy does not take into account the holiness of God or our need of the Cross. These will be discussed in chapter 4.
4. Karl Barth, *Church Dogmatics*, vol. II/2, authorized translation (Edinburgh: T. & T. Clark, 1957), p. 41.
5. A weakness in the analogy is that following God's law *does* improve our experience of life. The "law" we communicate to the fish won't help it much. The primary function of God's law, however, is the same: to alert us to our need for Him.
6. W. E. Vine, *Vine's Expository Dictionary of Old and New Testament Words* (Old Tappan, N.J.: Revell, 1981), p. 153.

Chapter 3

1. Paul Tournier, *The Meaning of Persons* (New York: Harper & Row Publishers, Inc., 1957), p. 27.
2. Everett L. Shostrom, *From Manipulator to Master* (New York: Bantam, 1983), pp. 1,2.
3. It's not my goal in this book to develop a theology of hell. I strongly encourage the reading of *The Great Divorce*, by C. S. Lewis. Hell is not something imposed on us by God, but it's the natural consequence of our insisting on being in control rather than trusting Him. We are judged by our own judgments. See Romans 1,2.
4. Claude Steiner, *Scripts People Live* (New York: Grove Press, 1974), pp. 176-85.

Chapter 4

1. C. S. Lewis, *The Lion, the Witch and the Wardrobe* (New York: Macmillan Publishing Co., 1950), p. 160.
2. C. S. Lewis, *The Problem of Pain* (New York: Macmillan Publishing Co., 1962), pp. 110,111.

Chapter 5

1. Claudia Black, *It Will Never Happen to Me* (Denver: M.A.C. Printing and Publications, 1981), pp. 28-49.
2. From *My Utmost for His Highest* by Oswald Chambers. Copyright © 1935, 1963 by Oswald Chambers Publications Assn., Ltd. Used by permission of Discovery House Publishers, Grand Rapids, MI 49501.
3. From *A Testament of Hope* by Thomas R. Kelly. Copyright 1941 by Harper & Row, Publishers, Inc. Copyright renewed ©1969 by Lois Lael Kelly Statler. Reprinted by permission of the Publisher.
4. Chambers, p. 12.
5. Chambers, p. 29.
6. The process of death and resurrection is not exclusively Christian. Many non-Christians experience a sense of new life when they face their pain and open their hearts. In groups such as AA and ACA, they do this by entrusting themselves to their "higher power." The secular therapist or philosopher might say I'm adapting a reality about all of life to Christian theology. In other words, he would say the death and resurrection we experience emotionally have nothing to do with the cross; they're just part of life. This secular perspective is logical but leaves open the question, Why are death and resurrection an integral part of life? Could it be they're part of the One who created it? Could it be, further, that all of nature reveals death and resurrection as a testimony to the reality and power of the cross, rather than that Christianity borrowed the concepts from nature?

The Christian perspective is that the cross was and is the central event of human history. Life becomes meaningful only through the cross. The fact that death and resurrection are a part of all creation, including the experience of non-Christians, should point us to the cross, not lead us to discount it. Nature is filled with death and resurrection as part of its testimony to Jesus Christ.

7. Chambers, p. 26.

Chapter 6

1. Taken from THE NIV STUDY BIBLE. Copyright 1985 by The Zondervan Corporation. Used by permission.
2. Adapted from Maurice Wagner as quoted in H. Norman Wright, *Training Christians to Counsel* (Denver: Christian Marriage Enrichment, 1977), p. 20.
3. Jesus' words imply a physical leaving of family as well. I don't believe, however, that He is calling us to abandon those we have committed ourselves to support. Rather, they are not to be gods to us. No doubt His disciples left spouses and children physically to follow Him, but it is contradictory to the rest of Scripture to assume He's calling us to abandon those who legitimately depend on us.

Chapter 7

1. Robert Farrar Capon, Episcopal Priest, Theologian and Food Writer, *Between Noon and Three* (San Francisco: Harper & Row Publishers, Inc., 1982), p. 148.
2. Capon, p. 100.
3. Earl F. Palmer, *Salvation by Surprise* (Dallas, Texas: WORD Incorporated, 1975).
4. Paul Tournier, *The Adventure of Living* (New York: Harper & Row Publishers Inc., 1965), p. 137.
5. Brendan Meehan as quoted in *The Wittenburg Door*, issue #93, October-November 1986, p. 13.
6. Tournier, p. 110.
7. Tournier, p. 159.
8. Dietrich Bonhoeffer, *Letters and Papers from Prison* (New York: Macmillan, 1953), p. 22.
9. From *My Utmost for His Highest* by Oswald Chambers. Copyright © 1935, 1963 by Oswald Chambers Publications Assn., Ltd. Used by permission of Discovery House Publishers, Grand Rapids, MI 49501.

Chapter 8

1. John Powell, *Why Am I Afraid to Tell You Who I Am?* (Niles, IL: Argus Communications, 1969), p. 12.
2. M. Scott Peck, *The Different Drum* (New York: Simon & Schuster, 1987), p. 59.
3. Janet Woititz has identified a number of myths that block intimacy. Many of

the beliefs I've identified are adaptations of hers. If you're interested in pursuing them, I recommend her book *Struggle for Intimacy*.
4. M. Scott Peck, *People of the Lie* (New York: Simon & Schuster, 1983), p. 269.
5. Ray Stedman, *Expository Studies in John 13-17* (Dallas, Texas: WORD Incorporated, 1975), p. 91.
6. C.S. Lewis, *The Voyage of the Dawn Treader* (London: Collins Publishers, 1952), pp. 75-76,88,90-91.
7. Of course, it often happens that one partner wants to love this way and his or her partner refuses. That's terribly painful. In that circumstance, it's usually difficult to distinguish between loving sacrificially and rescuing the partner from consequences he or she needs to experience. True love includes confronting attitudes and behaviors that are damaging, including another's refusal to love.

Chapter 9

1. Bellah, et al., *Habits of the Heart* (Berkeley: University of California Press, 1985), p. 142.
2. I recommend *Habits of the Heart*, by Bellah, Madsen, Sullivan, Swidler and Tipton, Harper and Row, 1985 for an in-depth examination of individualism and commitment in American life.
3. Taken from THE NIV STUDY BIBLE. Copyright 1985 by The Zondervan Corporation. Used by permission.
4. From *My Utmost for His Highest* by Oswald Chambers. Copyright © 1935, 1963 by Oswald Chambers Publications Assn., Ltd. Used by permission of Discovery House Publishers, Grand Rapids, MI 49501.
5. M. Scott Peck, *The Different Drum* (New York: Simon & Schuster, 1987), p. 59.
6. Ibid., p. 67.
7. Ibid., p. 75.
8. Elizabeth O'Connor, *Call to Commitment* (New York: Harper & Row Publishers Inc., 1963), p. 33.
9. Elizabeth O'Connor, *Journey Inward, Journey Outward* (New York: Harper & Row Publishers Inc., 1968), p. 24.
10. Ibid., pp. 36,37.
11. Ibid., p. 25.
12. Ibid., p. 40.
13. Parker J. Palmer, "Borne Again: The Monastic Way to Church Renewal," from *Weavings: A Journal of the Christian Spiritual Life*, September/October 1986 Copyright 1986 by The Upper Room. Reprinted by permission of Parker J. Palmer.
14. Ibid., p. 18.
15. Peck, pp. 103,104.
16. O'Connor, *Call to Commitment*, pp. 24,25.

17. Peck, p. 17.
18. O'Connor, *Journey Inward, Journey Outward*, p. 54.
19. Ibid., pp. 32,33.

RECOMMENDED READING

CHAPTER 1

There are many excellent books that can help in understanding the problem of shame and its effect on individuals and relationships. I recommend:

Bradshaw, John. *Healing the Shame That Binds You.* Deerfield Beach, FL: Health Communications, 1988.

Narramore, Bruce and Counts, Bill. *Guilt and Freedom.* Eugene, OR: Harvest House, 1974.

Whitfield, Charles L. *Healing the Child Within.* Pompano Beach, FL: Health Communications, 1987.

CHAPTER 2

If you're interested in pursuing an understanding of lies as a tool of evil, I recommend:

Lewis, C.S. *The Screwtape Letters.* New York: Macmillan Co., 1966.

Peck, M. Scott. *People of the Lie.* New York: Simon & Schuster, 1983.

CHAPTER 3

For further information on family roles and dysfunctional family patterns, I recommend the following books.

Family Roles

Black, Claudia. *It Will Never Happen to Me.* Denver, CO: MAC Pub., 1981.

Gravitz, Herbert L. and Bowden, Julie D. *Recovery.* New York: Simon & Schuster, 1987.

Satir, Virginia. *Making Contact.* Berkeley, CA: Celestial Arts, 1976.

Satir, Virginia. *Peoplemaking.* Palo Alto, CA: Science & Behavior Books, 1988.

Rescuer Role and Codependency

Beattie, Melody. *Codependent No More.* New York: Harper & Row, 1987.

Kiley, Dan. *The Wendy Dilemma.* New York: Avon, 1984.

Norwood, Robin. *Women Who Love Too Much.* Los Angeles, CA: J.P. Tarcher, 1985.

Victim Role

Kiley, Dan. *The Peter Pan Syndrome.*(male victim role) New York: Dodd, Mead, 1983.

Dowling, Colette. *The Cinderella Complex.* (female) New York: Simon & Schuster, 1981.

CHAPTER 4

Bright, John. *The Kingdom of God.* Nashville, TN: Abingdon Press, 1953.

Lewis, C.S. *The Problem of Pain.* New York: Macmillan, 1966.

Buechner, Frederick. *Telling the Truth.* New York: Harper & Row, 1977.

Lewis, C.S. *Mere Christianity.* New York: Macmillan, 1960.

CHAPTER 5

O'Connor, Elizabeth. *Cry Pain, Cry Hope.* Dallas: WORD Publishing, 1987.

CHAPTER 6

O'Connor, Elizabeth. *Search for Silence.* San Diego, CA: Lura Media, 1986.

Van Reken, Ruth E. *Letters Never Sent.* Elgin, IL: David C. Cook, 1988.

Tournier, Paul. *The Meaning of Persons.* New York: Harper & Row, 1965.

CHAPTER 7

Tournier, Paul. *The Adventure of Living.* New York: Harper & Row, 1965.

Capon, Robert Farrar. *Between Noon and Three.* New York: Harper & Row, 1982.

Peck, M. Scott. *The Road Less Traveled.* New York: Simon & Schuster, 1978.

CHAPTER 8

Woititz, Janet. *Struggle for Intimacy,* Pompano Beach, FL: Health Communications, 1985.

Powell, John. *Why Am I Afraid to Tell You Who I Am?* Niles, IL: Argus Communications, 1969.

Powell, John. *Why Am I Afraid to Love?* Niles, IL: Argus Communications, 1972.

Powell, John. *The Secret of Staying in Love.* Valencia, CA: Tabor Publishing, 1990.

CHAPTER 9

I have quoted extensively from Elizabeth O'Connor and Scott Peck because they have deeply influenced my understanding of community. I especially recommend these books:

O'Connor, Elizabeth. *Journey Inward, Journey Outward.* New York: Harper & Row, 1968.

Peck, M. Scott. *The Different Drum.* New York: Simon & Schuster, 1987.

Nouwen, Henri. *Reaching Out.* New York: Doubleday & Co., 1975.

O'Connor, Elizabeth. *Call to Commitment.* New York: Harper & Row, 1963.

If you're interested in further reading on community, I suggest you request reading lists from The Church on the Saviour and The Foundation for Community Encouragement at the addresses and phone numbers at the end of chapter 9.

Christ in You Seminars
led by Ken Schmidt

JESUS said "The truth will set you free," yet many Christians live in misery rather than freedom and joy. They feel depressed and trapped in lives with little hope. Though they take their faith seriously and try to obey Christ, they're not really alive.

We don't experience the joy, peace and power of Christ when we fail to grasp that He is alive within us. Our trust is usually in Christ as someone outside us who gives us rules to live by. This doesn't bring life! When we realize His Spirit is within and can be trusted, life becomes an adventure to be enjoyed.

I have developed Christ in You Seminars because I've discovered that *trusting Christ within you will change your life*. As you trust Him, you will grow stronger and more able to love and enjoy the gift of life.

Ken Schmidt

SCHEDULING A SEMINAR

If you would like to have one of the Christ in You Seminars presented to your church or organization contact Family Resources at (805) 652-2283. Ask for Ken Schmidt. Fees depend on the time desired, the location and the number of participants. Your organization's financial situation will also be considered in determining fees. If you prefer to write us our address is:

**Family Resources
2580 E. Main Street #201
Ventura, California 93003**

THE SEMINARS:

Breaking Free
Break free from dysfunctional family patterns and join the family of God.

Together to Grow
Marriage is an opportunity to mature in Christ.

Man to Man
To be a man we need other men.

Created from Within
Our children are being created by God, our role is to cooperate with Him.

**Hiding from Judgment
Hurting for Love**
It isn't God's judgment that's hurting us, it's our own!

Grace-full Sex
God's grace can free us to enjoy our sexuality.

Understanding the Men in Your Life
Men's issues and their effects on women.

FAMILY RESOURCES